AmericanHeritage®

Great Minds of History

AmericanHeritage®

GREAT MINDS OF HISTORY

Interviews by ROGER MUDD

Introduction by Richard Snow
Editor, *American Heritage*

John Wiley & Sons, Inc.
New York • Chichester • Weinheim • Brisbane • Singapore • Toronto

Copyright © 1999 by Unapix Entertainment, Inc., and American Heritage, a division of Forbes Inc. All rights reserved.
Published by John Wiley & Sons, Inc.
Published simultaneously in Canada

AMERICAN HERITAGE is a registered trademark of Forbes Inc. Its use is pursuant to a license agreement with Forbes Inc.

GREAT MINDS OF . . . is a trademark of Unapix Entertainment, Inc. Its use is pursuant to a license agreement.

Unapix Entertainment, Inc., and WGBH/Boston produced the television series on which this book is based. This series is sponsored by Travelers Group.

This publication is designed to provide accurate and authoritative information in regard to the subject matter covered. It is sold with the understanding that the publisher is not engaged in rendering professional services. If professional advice or other expert assistance is required, the services of a competent professional person should be sought.

Library of Congress Cataloging-in-Publication Data:

Mudd, Roger.
American Heritage great minds of history / interviews by Roger Mudd ; introduction by Roger Mudd ; introduction by Richard Snow.
p.   cm.
Includes bibliographical references and index.
ISBN 0-471-32715-8 (cloth : alk. paper)
1. United States—History.   2. Historians—United States—Interviews.   I. Title.   II. Title: Great minds of history.
E178.6.M89   1999
973—dc21   98-44710

Printed in the United States of America

10 9 8 7 6 5 4 3 2 1

Contents

AmericanHeritage®

Great Minds of History

Introduction: Talking History

Why read this book instead of their books?

After all, the five historians Roger Mudd interviews in this volume are at the very top of their profession, and their works—garlanded with prizes, some of them near-permanent fixtures on the best-seller lists—are the result of the most careful pruning and polishing, each the finished product of what in fact is a lifetime of application.

Well, of course you should read their books (and after reading this one, I think you'll be eager to), but these discussions offer something beyond the scope of their published works: an intimate immediacy, a sense of the fizz and crackle of events actually taking place.

For these men all live in the land where anything can happen: where the Federal troops a mile away from Pickett's brigade may not hold the low stone wall; where the brave words of the Declaration of Independence may end up being just that—brave summertime words that the Rebels finally cannot defend—and our nation an adjunct of Canada; where at the end of the day, Eisenhower pulls the troops off the Normandy beaches and takes the blame on himself. In a recent commencement address at the University of Massachusetts, Boston, David McCullough said: "It might never have happened. That's among the most important lessons of history—and of life. There is so much around us that might never have happened were it not for a host of qualities called imagination, commitment,

courage, creativity, and determination in the face of obstacles—that maybe most of all."

It is all too easy to see history as a sort of preordained path that dutiful, rather remote figures made
their way along—until, of course, that convenient path
ends in the labyrinth of threats and opportunities that
is the present. "You see it all the time," says David Mc-
Cullough in his interview in this book, "'Oh, that was a
simple time.' There *was* no simpler time. It may seem
simple to us, but it certainly didn't seem simple to
them."

This sense of all the untaken choices that once were
shining and beckoning gives the best historical writing
richness and tension, and gives these discussions much
of their savor. Every one of these historians is at home
in a past seething with possibilities. Did the Confederacy lose its last chance at Gettysburg? James McPherson doesn't think so. Here he is speaking about the
situation a full year later. "The peace wing of the Democratic Party looked like they probably would dominate
the Democratic convention. And indeed, for the most
part, did . . . Of course they said negotiation would bring
the South back into the Union, but nobody believed
that. Lincoln wrote a famous blind memorandum in
August 1864 saying that he was likely to lose the election." If he had, "there was a real chance the North
would just give up. Just as the United States finally decided to throw in the towel and negotiate a peace with
Vietnam in 1972 or 1973. And of course we say that the
North Vietnamese won that war because the United
States gave up and pulled out. If the United States—or
the Union—had given up and pulled out, as looked very
possible in the late summer of 1864, the Confederacy
would have won that war."

Hearing such speculation in the casual forum of a
conversation lends it an urgency that brings its mean-

ing closer to us. So, too, with the people who drove our history. Of course, it's a truism that history is made by men and women like you and me, but it is not always easy to connect our human volatility with, say, the pantheon of Founders, who have been transmogrifying themselves into bronze and marble vessels of inevitability for more than two centuries now. But listen to Gordon Wood, who has spent enough time with these people to know their foibles and impulses, their jealousies and little malevolences—in short, their humanity—and they come quite close: "Adams was most lovable of the Founding Fathers because he wore his heart on his sleeve . . . and his letters just spill out with his emotions. So any historian working on his papers comes to love him because he didn't hold anything back. Unlike Franklin, he's all out there, everything is there . . ."

Or, closer to our own time, here is Stephen Ambrose's tersely eloquent statement on what he likes about Eisenhower: "Listen, Roger, this is the best man that this country produced in this century—the most honest, the most trustworthy, the hardest-working, the most ambitious, the most decisive, the one who thought problems through better than anybody else, the best politician, and on and on and on." And on a colleague of Ike's that he doesn't like so well: "MacArthur—this sounds terrible, but it's true—MacArthur lied his way out of every difficulty he ever got into."

These interviews are full of such assessments, deeply felt and long considered yet delivered in the offhand give-and-take of conversation with a spontaneity that makes it seem as if the figures being discussed are living acquaintances. As, in a way, they are.

And these talks are full of surprises. Who, for instance, are the two people who have most shaped our current thinking about the American West? It may not be startling that one of the two Richard White cites is

INTRODUCTION

Frederick Jackson Turner, and in doing so gives this engaging summary of Turner's impact: "He framed the way that many Americans look at the world—even if they've never heard of Frederick Jackson Turner. I mean, that's the mark of a great historian: nobody even knows who you are, but they end up recapitulating most of what you'd said." The other one did startle me: William F. Cody. "The interesting thing about his story is that it's hard to say where the theater stops and real life begins. And Buffalo Bill was a master at that sort of postmodern West."

We know the Civil War killed a lot of Americans—600,000 of them. But James McPherson brought me up short with a simple calculation: "That was 2 percent of the American population of 1861. If 2 percent of the Americans were today to lose their lives in a war fought by this country, the number of American war dead would be five million." This goaded me into the only voluntary mathematical effort I've made since I got out of school. The Revolution is, I think, generally regarded as more a matter of politics than bloodshed: there was some picturesque musketry, and real strife, but in the main the quaint long-ago-ness of it kept the human carnage relatively low. I checked the battle deaths and carried out the arithmetic—and found that if the Revolution were fought today with the same percentage of causalities, it would leave two and a half million Americans dead. We bought our independence more dearly than I had understood.

Throughout these discussions I was ambushed by intriguing asides that made me look at the familiar through a slightly different lens. I think this may happen to you, too. And there are further dimensions to this book. Its discussions add up to an informal, wonderfully brisk history of the nation. Gordon Wood speaks about the Revolution and the republic it forged; Richard

White tells of the ways in which the West has shaped us all; James McPherson traces the coming of the Civil War, the conflict itself, and its aftermath; David McCullough summons up the immense vitality of what Kenneth Clark called the "age of heroic materialism," when Americans used the tools of the nineteenth century to build the twentieth; and Stephen Ambrose carries the story on through the calamity and triumph of World War II, the Cold War, and the endlessly fascinating dolors of the Nixon years to the present.

Cast in this unusual form, the narrative is always kinetic, darting, and oblique; and the narrators have at once too high and too close a regard for their subject to sentimentalize it. Nevertheless, the cumulative message is clear and heartening. There's a solemn pleasure to be taken in the fact that Ambrose, who has unflinchingly recorded the squalid rat-eat-rat maneuverings of Watergate—and, for that matter, American GIs shooting unarmed prisoners—can say, "These things happened and I report on them. But, regardless, this is the best country that ever was. This is the freest and, right now, the most prosperous that has ever been conceived anywhere. And, by God, somebody had to be doing something right to bring us to this point. I want to celebrate the people who brought us to this point."

I would like to thank the five writers who have given us so fresh and lively a summary of our shared past—and of course Roger Mudd, whose shrewd, knowledgeable questions reflect both his eminence as a journalist and his lifelong interest in the field that was very nearly his main calling. But should this expression of gratitude suggest I had any real role in the project, I'm perpetrating a fraud. These discussions were the idea of Tim Smith of Unapix, who brought them to the screen as a series broadcast in the fall of 1998, aided by the skills of his producer, Steve Atlas. Jeanette Baik and Christine

INTRODUCTION

Gibson of the *American Heritage* staff gathered research for the interviewer, and wrote the profiles of his subjects. Barbara Strauch, the director of Forbes and American Heritage book projects, mediated between us and the publisher with her usual competence and zeal. Even the most articulate of speakers (and these particular speakers are the most articulate) need some translation before their remarks can flow easily from speech to page; for this, my warmest thanks go to my colleague Catherine Calhoun, who took time from her duties as General Manager of American Heritage to edit the transcripts and in so doing made a fine television series into a fine book.

—Richard F. Snow
Editor, *American Heritage*

CHAPTER ONE

Gordon Wood
on the Colonial Era
and Revolution

Many consider America's struggle for independence a "conservative revolution"—no regicide, moderate bloodshed, no chaos. Gordon Wood, a foremost historian of the era, deems it "as radical and as revolutionary as any in history." In *The Radicalism of the American Revolution,* which won the 1993 Pulitzer Prize in history, Wood tells how the colonists erased the old social bonds (and chains) of patronage and blood aristocracy and replaced them with the first truly commercial society, thus becoming "almost overnight, the most liberal, the most democratic, the most commercially minded, and the most modern people in the world."

Wood's earlier book, *The Creation of the American Republic, 1776–1787,* won both the Bancroft and John H. Dunning prizes in history. A professor of history at Brown University, Wood is currently at work on a study of Benjamin Franklin, who, in his metamorphosis from blue-collar worker to rich, accomplished leader, is the exemplar of Wood's ideas on the early life of America.

———

Q: From time to time I read that George Washington was not the general we have come to believe he was— that he was, in fact, a second-rate general. What is your opinion?

A: Washington is a complicated figure. He certainly did not have a great military experience. He was a militia colonel who had had several engagements, most of which had been disastrous prior to 1760. But he was the one military person, particularly from the South, who had military experience and an international reputation for valor, at least.

It was important that he was from the South. With New England on the defensive, having led this assault against the Crown, it was necessary for New Englanders to show that Virginia supported this cause, too. So it was natural to look to a Virginian as the commander in chief. There were other people who probably had more, or at least equal, military skills, I suppose, but Washington turned out to be a superb choice.

He was not a great tactician; he was not a great general in that sense. But he had skills similar to Eisenhower's—political skills. He had the skills to hold an army together, and to keep diverse interests concentrated on the war. His skills made the war successful. And I believe they made him our greatest president.

Q: Do you think, Professor Wood, that your colleagues, professional historians, have done George Washington a disservice by making him such a mythical figure?

A: I don't think it's the professional historians that have made him a mythical figure.

Q: You don't?

A: I think it's been the popular culture. Of course, in the twentieth century he has become much less mythical. But in the nineteenth century, or in his own time, in fact, he was already recognized as the father of his country. And then with Parson Weems and the cherry tree myths, he became a superhero. And then some debunking came in the twentieth century.

I think most professional historians have been quite honest in their treatment of Washington. He is very difficult to penetrate because he's very reserved. He is so unlike our present public figures that one feels he comes from another world.

The presidents that came after him were all very different. Washington had different standards of leadership; he had different understandings of politics. He did not like the notion of political parties. He simply is a man from another time and another place.

Q: But he worked awfully hard himself at building up his own myth of Olympian stature, did he not? Wasn't he image conscious?

A: Very much so. He was concerned that he keep a certain distance from the populace, because he had this notion that that was what made for a good leader. So he didn't want to get too familiar. He was very self-conscious about that. He was not ashamed of being an elitist. He didn't use that term, but he certainly had no embarrassment about his superior station in life.

He had an international reputation right away in 1783, after he resigned his commission. He surrendered his sword to the Congress, and that was the greatest act of his life, by the way. That's what gave him this international reputation.

Q: Why was that the greatest?

A: Because the expectation that everyone had was that a victorious general would have political rewards commensurate with his military victories, that he would go on to have political success. But instead, Washington promised that he would return to Mount Vernon. He promised the people that he would retire from active, public life. That's why he was so reluctant to come out of retirement to go to the Constitutional Convention. And then he was even more reluctant to accept the presidency, because he felt he would be going back on his word. He said, "What will the people think? What will this do for my reputation?" He took that very, very seriously.

Q: So what is it about Washington that makes him, as you describe him, our greatest president?

A: A number of things. He had the hardest job because he was the first. He had precedents to set, and he knew that. He was a natural leader who worked at it at the same time. And he had that ability to command.

As I said, I think the closest we've come to that in modern times would be Eisenhower. Now, Eisenhower may not have been a great general in any kind of traditional sense, but he had a certain quality of leadership that people can appreciate. He had an ability to bring people together and keep them focused on the cause.

And Washington also had that to a great degree. He just had the ability to command the respect of those around him.

Q: Does that mean that his moral fiber was stronger and tougher than anybody since?

A: He certainly was conscious of moral qualities. What is the right thing to do? What will command respect? He thought about that all the time, he worried about it. He was simply an extraordinary man in that respect.

Q: What was the significance of George Washington's decision in 1796 to retire from the presidency?

A: Actually, he wanted to retire in 1792, but nobody would let him. He really felt that he'd love to get back to Mt. Vernon. In fact, I think he was really pressured into the job in the first place. In 1792 he was sure he was going to go back home, but he got enormous pressure from everyone—from Madison, from Hamilton, from some women who wrote wonderful letters to him: "Mr. Washington, you must stay in office because the whole government depends on you." So he stayed in, very reluctantly. And by 1796 he simply had to go. He had to leave because the criticism had become very, very intense. The press was writing really vicious stuff that makes our media today seem very, very tame by comparison. Washington was just discouraged, and he knew he had to get back to Mt. Vernon.

Q: Why was the press so critical of him? What was happening?

A: There was a growing rift between the elite and the rest of the country. It seemed as if the whole government was at stake. The Republicans, led by Jefferson, felt that the Federalists, who were in charge of the government, were attempting to turn the United States into a monarchy. They truly believed that. It wasn't just a phrase they used rhetorically.

And it was a kind of politics that we simply haven't seen since in our history, except perhaps on the eve of the Civil War. The country was really torn in passionate antagonisms. So Washington was caught in the middle of this. He kept holding this cabinet together, first with Hamilton and Jefferson, and then in the end, he was really holding the country together. Finally, he knew he had to get out of that turmoil.

Q: Was it a serious possibility that all of those trappings of the monarchy could have become part of American democracy?

A: I don't think it was, no. I don't think the country was going to become a monarchy. There was too much pressure going in the opposite direction. But there were Federalists who were concerned about what they would have called "wild democracy," and they thought that monarchy, or at least a little bit of monarchy, was essential to restrain it. In fact, the president was designed as a kind of elected king right from the beginning. It's a very powerful office, as we know; we've seen it develop without any great Constitutional changes.

So there was a monarchical impulse inherent in the presidency when the Constitution was drawn up in 1787. But Washington was not a monocrat himself, and he liked the title "Mr. President"—unlike John Adams, who wanted "his high mightiness" or some other kind of elaborate monarchical title. After all, governors were called "his excellency"—why shouldn't the president have had something more elaborate than "Mr. President"? John Adams was astonished at the simplicity of that title.

Q: Let's talk about the Revolution. Do you think the colonies were lucky to have won?

A: Lucky is perhaps not the right word. They had an awful lot of luck, I suppose. But in the end, it wasn't just luck—it was a widespread support for the Revolution in the population that made it possible. And there was also the French aid. There is no doubt that the French intervention changed the nature of the war and put England in an impossible position. She was suddenly fighting a world war with no allies. And that made the colonies' success much more likely.

Q: Do you think the colonists were justified in revolting?

A: Well, I would have to say they were. Certainly, the British showed very little political sense of what the colonies had, how they had developed in the previous century. So they bungled the relationship; there is no doubt of that.

Q: But were the conditions in the colonies truly suffi-cient to have produced a revolution? I mean, were the conditions described by the Declaration of Indepen-dence in fact the conditions that existed? Was there tyranny? Was there oppression? Was there despotism?

A: Well, no. By any kind of modern standards, there was no tyranny at all. The British simply had not had any kind of power over the colonies. So this was an exagger-ation by Jefferson. But there was the anticipation of tyranny. The Americans revolted out of anticipated tyranny, rather than actual tyranny. They were frightened about the use of power. If the British Parliament could do what it had done in the previous decade, with the Stamp Act and so on, what would it do in the future? That, I think, is what led to the rebellion and revolution.

Q: The slogan "taxation without representation" is not much of a battle cry, is it?

A: Well, "taxation without representation" was only one of the elements. The true cause was liberty and a sense of freedom—freedom from a government three thousand miles away dictating decisions over which the colonists had no say. Freedom was the crucial issue.

Q: When the colonists talked about freedom, what was their definition of freedom? Was it the same as ours?

A: Generally, yes; except, of course, they didn't neces-sarily apply it to the five hundred thousand slaves. How-

ever, there is no doubt the Revolution created a con-
sciousness of liberty, of freedom that suddenly made
slavery a problem where it hadn't been a problem before.
So their notions of freedom are not all that different
from our own notions today.

Q: I had always understood that when they talked
about freedom, they talked about freedom from domination by someone else. But more recently, you hear
about freedom to get a job, freedom from want. Is that
our definition of freedom?

A: Well, those are FDR's freedoms. Obviously, the colonists didn't have a welfare state conception. They
didn't feel that the government had a responsibility to
provide for a citizen's welfare. But they certainly had all
kinds of private concerns within eighteenth-century
standards. There were lots of philanthropic endeavors
that came out of the Revolution—humanitarian societies, anti-slave societies—a whole host of things that
we can understand today as acts of compassion, having
to do with a larger definition of freedom. But they were
not socialists—they didn't have the twentieth-century
notions of government responsibility that we take for
granted today.

Q: What was the nature of the Revolution itself? It
wasn't barbaric like the French Revolution, was it? It
didn't have the violence and the societal overthrow and
turmoil that many revolutions have had. Was it kind of
an intellectual revolution?

A: Yes, it was an intellectual revolution, but it was a

social revolution as well. It doesn't have the violence of the French Revolution, which had to do with a breakdown in the elite's control of things.

However, there was violence in the American Revolution. There were Tories who were harried out of the land. There were Loyalists who were hanged in some cases, and their property was confiscated in other cases. But they were a tiny minority, and they weren't strong enough in most cases to mount any great opposition. So there wasn't any escalation of emotions and violence as there was in the French Revolution.

Q: What did the English make of this revolution? Did the English Crown understand what was happening in the colonies?

A: Yes, they did. George III was very frightened about what was happening, and he was really resistant to any kind of concession toward the end. And, to a large degree, his unwillingness to concede created the rebellion.

He had what we today would call a domino theory: Lord North, his prime minister, came to him in 1779 or 1780 and said, "Sir, we cannot continue this fight. It's not going anywhere. It's costing us too much." North gave a kind of cost-benefit analysis of what was happening. And George III said to him, "No, if we lose the colonies, next will be Ireland, and then what will this poor little island be like?" He saw a series of events following from the loss of the colonies that would diminish Great Britain.

But, of course, the opposite happened. Britain went on to its greatest days as an empire in the nineteenth century. But he couldn't have foreseen this. He thought he was going to go down in history as the king who had lost the empire.

Gordon Wood

Q: Weren't the colonists also revolting against European monarchies and that whole life of luxury and domination?

A: The transition to republicanism from monarchy was a major and radical step. And, in that sense, the revolt against the English king was the revolt against the whole notion of monarchy, yes. The adoption of a republican government resulted in a simpler, more egalitarian society. So you might say it was a rejection of the old world, and this new younger world represented the future. That was the way in which they saw the Revolution.

It was not just an ordinary colonial rebellion. It was a real historical event that was presaging the future. That this was going to happen everywhere. Everyone was going to become republican. The world was going to lose this older monarchical society, which was identified, as you say, with luxury, with corruption.

So it had much more meaning than simply another colonial rebellion, of which there have been many in history.

Q: Did the colonists know what they had done when they did it?

A: Well, insofar as anyone participating in an event understands what's happening, they did. They understood the significance of it. They were told that it was significant by radical intellectuals everywhere. Richard Price in England, a well-known Unitarian radical minister, said at the time that the American Revolution was the most important event in the history of the world after the birth of Christ.

So there was a sense everywhere in the Western

world among liberal radical elements that this was a world-shattering event. And the Americans themselves believed that. That was part of the excitement, this enthusiasm they had about what they were doing.

Q: Do you believe that the Revolution is the most important single event in American history at least?

A: Oh, there's no doubt about it. It created the United States. It infused into our culture almost everything we believe: our noblest aspirations, our beliefs in liberty and equality. All of these things that we think of as the American ideology, the American principles—they came out of the Revolution.

Q: But it wasn't a foregone conclusion that democracy and liberty and equality were going to take hold. After all, the Founding Fathers all came from a fairly thin upper class, did they not?

A: They did.

Q: Were they really interested in equality and egalitarianism? I thought they had a low view of mechanics and artisans and those below them.

A: By eighteenth-century standards, they had actually a quite magnanimous view of ordinary people. Now it's true that they didn't think that carpenters and artisans and mechanics should be governors. But they thought that the sons of artisans could go on to Princeton or Harvard or some other college to become a gentleman and then become a leader. So they were in favor of what we would call upward mobility, social mobility. And in that sense they were quite radical for the age.

Q: You've mentioned many times the word *republicanism*. What was the definition of republicanism?

A: Well, the strict definition of it was a government that was elected. But in our Revolution it was more than that. It defined a world in which a person was measured by what he accomplished. What his ancestry was, what his genealogy was—these things didn't count as much as personal achievement. The phrase "republic of letters" was often used then, even by monarchists, and it meant that the world of arts and sciences was a world where only merit counted. As Thomas Paine said, who remembers Homer's father or Homer's son?

Republicanism had all of those connotations of a world of equality in that sense. Equality of opportunity, equality based on who you were, not on where you came from. Those were republican principles.

Q: Did it also involve the notion that disinterested men of virtue would work for the public good rather than the private gain?

A: The central premise was that every leader would be virtuous. The early Americans often used the term *disinterested* as a synonym for virtue. By that they meant "impartial"; they didn't mean "uninterested." They felt that there are people who have personal interests but are able to overcome them and make decisions for the good of society. And that was central to the republican notion of leadership.

Q: So what happened to get us to our present circumstances?

A: What happened, I suppose, was that that kind of vision couldn't be sustained. I think we still have a hope that our leaders will be disinterested. But we also understand that politics is about the competition of interests, and we now expect special interests to have a role in government. We understand lobbyists—we expect them to lobby for their cause. And we hope, as Madison put it, that there will be enough interests contending with one another that somehow out of all of the scramble something good will emerge. That's the modern democratic vision.

Q: If Madison and Jefferson and Franklin could look at our present society, they'd be sorely disappointed, would they not?

A: Probably. This isn't the world they wanted. I don't think the Founding Fathers expected quite as much democratic scrambling—the kind I just mentioned— as has emerged. In fact, very quickly some of them who lived into the nineteenth century were quite disillusioned. Jefferson, for example, was very disillusioned at the end of his life to see what had happened. And

Washington was very disillusioned by the time he died in 1799. But that's the problem of history. Change goes on relentlessly, and that's why older people tend to get disillusioned with their present—it's simply different from what they knew.

Now, was the world of the nineteenth century worse than that of the eighteenth? By no means. In many respects it was much better: There was an anti-slave movement that was going to eventually abolish slavery. There were women's movements. There was a whole host of things that were good and were part of democratic politics—and that the Founders hadn't anticipated.

Q: Would you say that the Founders would now regard their revolution as a failed revolution?

A: No. I think they would be quite pleased to see that two hundred years later, the country they created is still around. In fact, Washington was reported to have said when he came out of the Constitutional Convention, "This thing won't last twenty years." So I think they would be proud that it has lasted. And if they could study our history, they might very well think, "It hasn't done so badly after all."

Q: What was colonial society like a couple of hundred years ago?

A: Very different from our own, of course. It was a hierarchical world held together largely through patronage. And it was a small-scale society by our standards. By 1760 the total number of urban people was probably only sixty thousand to seventy thousand. That includes the six leading towns, ranging from Boston to Charleston. So it's a small-scale society deposited in a strip along the Atlantic coast, probably no more than two hundred miles inland.

It was a society with lots of unfree labor—both in the form of indentured servants and, of course, black slaves everywhere, not just in the South, although they dominated the South. But there were slaves in the North, as well, prior to the Revolution. There were about half a million African American slaves in total.

Q: How was slavery regarded in the colonies?

A: Well, it's important to understand that slavery was taken for granted in the Western world for centuries up through the eighteenth century, and this was also true in the colonies. There were some protests, and the number of protests would grow, particularly after the Revolution. But prior to the Revolution, there was relatively little criticism. There were some anti-slavery Quakers, whose importance has been exaggerated. But by and large, most people did not see the institution as an aberration, as something they should be embarrassed about. That's key to understanding the importance that the Revolution had on anti-slave thinking.

Q: And at that time there was slavery all over the world?

A: Not slavery, but unfreedom everywhere.

Q: Unfreedom?

A: Meaning white servants. A white servant could be bought and sold, and he could not own property. His life was not his own. Now, white servants didn't serve for life, except in some cases if they were prisoners. And they didn't pass the status on to their children as black slaves did. But there was a widespread sense that unfreedom existed everywhere, and therefore the peculiar unfreedom of the blacks was not as conspicuous as it would become later, when all white males became citizens.

Q: Who was maintaining the hierarchical society?

A: In English society, it ranged from the king down through the various members of the aristocracy—the nobility down through gentry—to the ordinary people and the various levels of unfreedom. The bottom rung was being an African slave in the colonies.

Q: So the gentry is the lowest level of the upper level.

A: Yes. The distinction between a gentleman and a commoner was much more conspicuous to eighteenth-century people than the line that we find so horrible: between the free and the enslaved. That line between who was and who was not a gentleman was a real and very important one. Probably 5 to 1 percent of the population was constituted gentry or gentlemen. And it was a very distinctive position.

Q: Were men able to move upward, through that line, or not?

A: People could move up, and they would pass. They used the term, "He's passing as a gentleman." To be a gentleman, of course, you had to maintain that status. You had to dress a certain way and have a certain amount of money to bring it off. But more importantly, you had to have a certain carriage, you had to have a certain ability to talk.

There is a fascinating journal of a Maryland physician in the 1740s who went up the Atlantic coast. He went everywhere, describing the society, and he found people who were passing as gentlemen. And he loved to expose their false status by talking Latin to them. Then the poor man who was passing as a gentleman was exposed as a fraud. This kind of interest—who is a gentleman, who is not—was central to the age.

Q: In colonial churches, particularly in the South, I know there were sections set aside for the commoners and, of course, the gallery for the slaves. Then the gentry came in as a group, didn't they?

A: The males would come in with their spurs jangling off as a group. With their wives already seated, they would come in as a display of authority, of power. There were lots of displays of authority. After all, there were no police forces. By modern standards, they had very few institutions to discipline people. So they built up these rituals so that people believed in deferring to their betters. And this was one way of displaying one's power and keeping order in the community.

Q: After independence, were the common folk really any closer to the gentry, the aristocracy, than they had been before independence?

A: Republicanism had implications of equality that changed things radically in time. You have to understand that for thousands of years there was this basic dichotomy in all Western cultures between an aristocracy, or however you want to describe them, and commoners. And those commoners didn't count for much in the workings of history.

That did change radically in the years following the Revolution. And it changed not just in America, of course, but the Western world in general. Intervening in this basic dichotomy was a third group that was often referred to in the eighteenth century as the "middling element." And this was an anticipation of what we would call the middle class. These middling sorts were artisans, businessmen, traders, and merchants who were making a lot of money and had a lot of self-esteem but who were not considered gentlemen. They had their own agendas, they had their own pride—particularly pride in work. They weren't ashamed to make money, which, of course, was always considered to be something that a gentleman couldn't do, not openly at least. These people were making themselves felt increasingly throughout the course of the eighteenth century. And it's their emergence in the early nineteenth century that brings us into modern society, into a world that we find recognizable.

This group was not really anticipated by the Founding Fathers. They didn't expect these artisans, these businessmen, to be politically dominant. And I think the most important social thrust of the Revolution was the emergence of this so-called middle class or middling element. They made a different kind of statement in the early nineteenth century about what life ought to be like.

Q: So then by 1810 or 1820, the middling element was the dominant group in America?

A: I would say so. I suppose one could argue that the gentry were still in control, certainly in the South. But in the North there had been a fundamental shift. By that time, even if you were a gentleman, you had to think of yourself as a worker like any other business-man, like any old printer or trader. You could not dis-parage ordinary people and their labor in the way that you might have done a hundred years earlier.

Now, the South remained much more traditional. The presence of slavery helped to guarantee that. And there was still an antagonism toward work and a much more traditional genteel attitude toward the society in general than the attitude found in the North at that time.

Q: If the Founding Fathers didn't anticipate the rise of the middling element, then how did it happen?

A: It resulted from social and economic developments. The society was becoming richer and wealthier, and these people were the productive source of the society. They were making money, doing very well for them-selves, and now they had several choices. They had the choice that Benjamin Franklin had: In 1747 he was a very wealthy printer. As long as he was a printer setting type, he could never be a gentleman. But once he decided in 1747 at the age of forty-two to retire (an early age for retirement), he was able to become a gentleman.

Q: Just like that?

A: Just like that. It was a very self-conscious and a conspicuous decision. He was wealthy enough to devote himself to public service, to science, to philosophy, which is what gentlemen could do. He couldn't be seen setting type any longer, because he couldn't be a businessman and a gentleman simultaneously.

What happened with many other wealthy businessmen later was that they refused to make this transition. They said, "I'm going to remain as a businessman and still be a gentleman." And they began to defend their work, their busy-ness, as something legitimate that didn't take away from their gentility. They claimed the status of gentlemen, without giving up their businesses.

That certainly didn't happen overnight. We still have the character of Silas Lapham at the end of the nineteenth century, who is worried about the fact that in Brahmin Boston he's not really quite a gentleman because he's too much of a businessman. So it was a long-term transition. And in some places today, in England I suppose, being in trade is still not quite right.

Q: But back to Benjamin Franklin, did he dress and speak like a gentleman?

A: That's exactly what happened. There is a portrait of him that isn't often seen—it's in the Fogg Museum at Harvard—and I would call it a coming-out portrait. He had it painted by Robert Feke, and in it he clearly looks like an aristocrat, not like the printer.

So he dressed accordingly and acted accordingly. There were, of course, people who always remembered that he had never been to college—and a liberal arts education became an increasingly important attribute of a gentleman. A college education at Princeton or Harvard was a ticket to gentility. Yet there were gentlemen like Washington and Franklin who had not attended college, and Washington at least was always embarrassed about it.

Q: And those businessmen who simply declared themselves to be gentlemen, there wasn't anybody to challenge them?

A: In the South there were plenty of people to expose or challenge them, and perhaps there were attempts made in the North. But this new breed was successful because they had so much wealth that they were able to force the gentry, the older gentry, to either remain quiet or go along with their standards. There was a marvelous episode with Edward Everett, who was a traditional Boston gentleman, governor, and senator. In the 1820s he was talking to a workingman's group and he told them, "I'm as much of a workingman as you are," and he defended labor. He blurred the distinction between manual labor and intellectual labor, which had never been done before. He lumped himself in with all workers, all laborers—everybody who worked for a living.

This is what foreign visitors found so surprising. When he first came here, Tocqueville was startled to realize that, in the North at least, nobody was ashamed of working. He said, "A French aristocrat would never admit that he was busy making money. But in America they don't seem to be embarrassed by that." That was part of the radicalism of the Revolution.

Q: So the middle class pulled down the aristocracy and lifted up the common class?

A: I think that's a good way of describing it.

Q: What role did the evangelical Christian movement play in the development of modern American society?

A: It obviously played a crucial role in developing the kind of Protestant Christianity that would characterize America. It began with the Puritans in the seventeenth century but really got its start in the Great Awakening of the mid-eighteenth century. Then it took off in a modern sense with the Revolution and the subsequent development of Protestant sects like the Baptists and the Methodists.

One has to understand that in the 1760s there were no Methodists in the colonies. By 1790 the Methodists had become the second-largest denomination. And by 1810 they were the largest denomination in America and growing rapidly. So they seemed to come out of nowhere. It was a similar story with the Baptists. There were Baptists here, of course, in 1760, but by no means did they dominate the culture. The dominant churches at that time were the Anglican, the Congregational, the Independents in New England, and the Presbyterians.

By 1810 it was the Methodists, the Baptists, and then the Presbyterians. So we had this enormous change in a relatively short period of time, only thirty or forty years, with evangelical Christianity. There was now a recognizably modern kind of Christianity—one that preached salvation for lots of people, not just to an elect. Calvinism—the notion that there are some people saved but not everyone—was on the defensive. These new preachers held out the promise of everybody being saved.

This kind of popular religion captured control of the culture to an extraordinary extent by the 1820s and '30s, without support by the state. There was the freedom of religion and the separation of church and state occurring at the very moment that there was this explosion of religious energy. It's all part of this middle-class rise that I mentioned earlier, because these people brought their religiosity with them.

You find that, in the eighteenth century, people, including the gentry, were generally lukewarm or even contemptuous about religious enthusiasm. But in the early nineteenth century, they can't afford to be publicly. There was just an extraordinary transformation of the culture in the early nineteenth century, which we call the second Great Awakening.

Q: I gather that it went hand in hand with the rise of the capitalist middle class, did it not?

A: Exactly. There was no incompatibility. In fact, I think the religion was important in disciplining the rise of capitalism. It controlled it; it kept it in wraps. It prevented the kind of wild capitalism that we can see occurring in other parts of the world today.

Q: We never learn very much about the anti-Federalists. It seems everything is written about the activists and not the opponents. Why is that?

A: Well, they were the losers in the debate over ratification of the Constitution. The anti-Federalists were the party that opposed the adoption of the Constitution in 1787 and 1788, and they lost that struggle. Although in the larger scheme of things, over the next generation, their heirs—the Republican party of Jefferson—actually won, at least temporarily. Now, in the twentieth century the Federalists have come back with the idea of a strong central state, and Hamilton would be very pleased.

But the anti-Federalists had really nothing to offer, except their opposition. They had no positive program. And when the Continental Congress or the Confederation Congress simply collapsed, the alternative was stark. As one anti-Federalist astutely put it: "It's this"—meaning the Constitution—"or nothing." And in the end most people couldn't accept the fact that there would be nothing, that this grand experiment would just fall apart.

So in the end, even some of the most devout anti-Federalists, like Melancton Smith in New York, voted for the Constitution. He realized that he wasn't going to support anarchy and the breakup of the union, so he reluctantly supported the Constitution.

But they had one big issue: the lack of a Bill of Rights in the original Constitution. And they applied enough pressure that the need for a Bill of Rights became widely accepted. Madison took it quite seriously. He promised in his election to the Congress in 1788 that as soon as he got into office, he would work toward amending the Constitution with a Bill of Rights. And he did so.

So that was the anti-Federalists' contribution to the struggle.

Q: But did Madison do that because he believed there ought to be a Bill of Rights? Or did he do it because he had to have the votes of the anti-Federalists?

A: Originally, he didn't feel the need for a Bill of Rights. He felt, with some justification, that writing down some specific rights might create the impression that these were the only rights. But he came around to believing that this list of rights was important.

Q: I'm always amazed to read the Constitution and find that it really is just a set of instructions, isn't it? I mean, there is not an awful lot there to tell the new men that are in power what to do.

A: It's a very short document when you think about it.

Q: These men were creating a whole new world and yet nobody knew exactly how to proceed, did they?

A: That's why Washington was so important— because he knew that. He said, "I am setting precedents every day." That's why he was so cautious, so careful, and so concerned. And, of course, the Constitution as we practice it has been filled in by two centuries of habit—

two centuries of practices and customs. I think it's foolish to think that those few words that are written down are all we use to govern ourselves with.

Q: Were the men who wrote the Constitution really brilliant, or did they just happen to luck into this new form?

A: They were certainly smart. I won't say that they were more brilliant than any other array of talent. Remember, they didn't have to defer to the people in the way that our politicians do. They didn't have democratic politics in that sense. After all, the Constitutional Convention was held in secret, with armed guards at the door. No press was allowed. The participants took a vow that they would not talk to the press. And that lasted about three or four months. Everyone knew they were meeting to create this Constitution, and they had taken oaths that they would not talk to anybody outside about what went on there.

That would not happen today; it's impossible.

Q: No leaks back then?

A: No, there were no leaks. In fact, Washington discovered a rough copy of the Constitution that they had had printed up to work on. And he held it up and said, "Somebody has left this on the desk." In other words, they hadn't guarded it. And he looked around and said, "I'll leave it here for the culprit to pick it up." But, of course, nobody did claim it, because they were too embarrassed to admit that they had done that.

So they took this very seriously. Madison said the Constitution could never have been created if it had been a public arena. The ratification was held in public. And it's interesting when you compare the debates in the two places. During the Constitutional Convention, they often talked about democracy in negative terms—wild democracy, the excesses of democracy—and the people were often disparaged—"the people run wild," and so on. But when they got to the ratifying conventions, at which the public was present, the rhetoric was "The people are glorious, the people are wonderful; all power to the people."

So there was a stark contrast. One should think about that when we talk about opening things to the public—courts or whatever. The participants are going to say different things.

Q: When the nation began to operate under the Constitution, was it assumed that the new president would serve one term after another? What did they think about presidential succession?

A: They were unsure of that. Everyone accepted the strong president that they had written into the Constitution because they knew Washington would be that president. And it was assumed by many people that Washington would serve for life. That is to say, he would be continually reelected as president.

Q: Who assumed that?

A: I think Jefferson, in fact, thought the president

would serve for life. He was not unhappy about Washington, because he felt he was a moderate man, but he worried about his successors. In fact, there was a good deal of concern all around. This was an unprecedented office—an office that had all of the potential power of the monarch. So there was a good deal of concern.

Q: What about the relationship between the Supreme Court and the Constitution? Was it envisioned that the Court would serve as the arbiter about Constitutional issues?

A: There is a good deal of confusion about that. I don't think anyone fully foresaw what has developed, particularly in the twentieth century, with judicial review. They knew that the court would have a certain amount of power and they wanted the court to be independent. But the growth of the independent judiciary over the next generation, particularly under the leadership of Marshall, was not clearly foreseen by the founders.

Q: So this is the first time in the history of the world that a people got their hands on a government, as opposed to a monarch.

A: It was certainly the first time in modern history, and they knew it. They were very self-conscious about that. They said no people in modern times has ever been able to make its own government in the way we have.

The original stage of the Revolution was the drafting of the state constitutions, the thirteen state constitutions, which they thought would be all they'd need to draft. Then they had the Articles of Confederation, which was a kind of European Union–like confederation, and they thought that would be enough. In 1776 nobody anticipated the kind of central government that was created in 1787. This came out of the disillusionment and the failure of the Confederation.

So having done this ten years later, the legislators felt they had a remedy. They had shown how people can diagnose their problems and prescribe a remedy and solve their problems with government all by themselves. This was really quite extraordinary, and that, I think, gave them enormous confidence.

So they headed into the 1790s with this tremendous sense of confidence that they were in control of their own destiny.

Q: What more can you tell me about Benjamin Franklin?

A: Well, Franklin is one of the most—if not the most—fascinating Founding Fathers of all. He came out of this really obscure background, an artisan background, and rose to the heights of the world. At the time of the Revolution, he was probably the most internationally famous of the Founding Fathers. Washington came in a close second.

But Franklin became a world-renowned scientist. And he made scientific discoveries in electricity beyond the gadgets we associate him with. It wasn't just the lightning rod or the Franklin stove. He made theoretical contributions to the understanding of electricity that electrified the world, if you will. He really was a distinguished philosopher and scientist, and that's where his reputation starts.

He was a man completely in control of himself. He played various roles, and therefore people never knew where they stood with him.

He is probably the most symbolic figure in all of American history, because he was later embraced by these rising middle-class artisans that I've mentioned, these businessmen, as their hero. In the 1810s and '20s, none of the other Founding Fathers could really be their hero. Jefferson was a slaveholder; John Adams was too aristocratic; Washington was too severe and remote. But Franklin was one of them. He was a former printer. So they made him their folksy hero.

Now, he wasn't that kind of a hero in his own lifetime, but he was a man who was often used in symbolic ways. But he's so reticent himself, even in the autobiography, that it's hard to know where he fully stands on many issues.

He was full of irony and a wonderful storyteller — an extraordinary man.

Q: What about Alexander Hamilton?

A: Hamilton was the brilliant genius of the Founding Fathers. He was the smartest of all of them. He matched Napoleon in sheer genius. I mean, he went through King's College at Columbia in just a matter of months when everyone else was taking years. He could read something and grasp it like that. He could write pungent, clear prose. And he understood banking and finance as none of the other Founding Fathers did. John Adams said, "I don't understand how money can be created. How can you have a piece of paper that is in excess of the gold and silver that is in the vault?" It had to be one-for-one as far as he was concerned, but Hamilton knew better.

He was short but attractive. He'd walk into a room and he would capture everyone's attention because he just had that kind of charisma.

Q: What can you tell us about James Madison?

A: Madison was the most intellectual, I think. He was also very short—and shy, not a dynamic person. Although, when he talked, people said he was a master of what he was talking about. He didn't have any great rhetorical ability, but people listened because they knew he had done his homework. And he had a theoretical understanding of the Constitution that was matched by almost none. I think James Madison was the only one who had a sense of what this system was like as a whole.

And Madison is certainly the most important figure in creating the Constitution and in creating the government. He was the most important member of the House. At one point, he wrote the response to the president's address—but of course he had written the president's address as well. President Washington would come to him and say, "Mr. Madison, you must write my inaugural address" or "my speech to the Congress." So Madison would, and then the House said to him, "You've got to write the response to the president." So he was writing responses to his own prose.

He was really an extraordinary man.

Q: John Adams?

A: Adams was the most lovable of the Founding Fathers because he wore his heart on his sleeve. He had this extraordinary diary, and his letters just spill out with his emotions. So any historian working on his papers comes to love him because he didn't hold anything back. Unlike Franklin, he's all out there, everything is there.

He was ineffectual at times, but at crucial moments there was no doubt of his patriotism. He wanted to do the right thing, and he made that extraordinary move to send a mission to France to head off a conflict, even though it got him into terrible trouble with his own Federalist party. And that really caused him to lose the 1800 election to Jefferson. But it was a patriotic act.

Q: And what do you think about Thomas Jefferson?

A: There is no doubt that Jefferson is the most important of the Founding Fathers, because he said everything that we've come to believe. He was the spokesman for democracy. But, for that reason, today he is certainly the most controversial. Because here you have an aristocrat who never freed his slaves, speaking out these great principles of liberty. "All men are created equal." And yet here he was violating that in his own lifetime. In a sense, he represents what a lot of historians feel is the hypocrisy of American life. He's come under tremendous criticism in the last thirty years.

But there is no doubt that he was the spokesman for democracy. His confidence in the people seemed unbounded. When Madison would talk about the people, he'd say, "Yes, the people but—." He would always qualify it. But Jefferson had more confidence. He said, "The people are good and they will see us through." And those are the kinds of statements we want to believe today. Those are the ones that get engraved on temples. Madison's qualifications just don't work.

Q: As a historian, what do you think about the use of contemporary standards of behavior and applying them to the way people behaved 150 and 200 years ago. Is that fair to them? After all, Jefferson is a victim of that, is he not?

A: Well, yes, of course. Obviously, it is an anachronism when you apply present-day standards to the past, but it's understandable to some degree. After all, we live in the present and we're interested in the past insofar as it somehow tells us how we came to be. So there is a present-mindedness, you might say, that is inherent in historical reconstruction.

But at the same time, there have got to be degrees of this kind of thing, or else you end up with an anachronistic account. If you're going to judge the Puritans, for example, by standards of toleration and religious liberty, then they're going to be seen as a bunch of bigots. In fact, in the 1890s, the Puritans of the seventeenth century were seen as a group of prejudiced, bigoted people who hanged Quakers on Boston Common. Well, it took a whole series of historians to recover the seventeenth-century Puritan experience in a historical way.

We're going through the same thing with the Founding Fathers now because many of them were slaveholders. And yet they spouted notions of liberty. I can understand that as a historian, but it's very difficult to communicate that to a modern audience. Students simply find that inconsistency intolerable. How can slaveholders talk about liberty without being hypocritical?

And I suppose in the end they were. Although it's important to understand that they knew they were doing wrong. That's very different from their predecessors, their earlier generations. They wrestled with this problem.

This is an impossible problem in today's climate. I've had students say, "There is no way the American Revolution could be seen as a success unless it abolished slavery entirely." And all I can say in response is that it did abolish slavery in the North, and it put the South so much on the defensive that it led inexorably to the Civil War. So the Revolution created the climate that eventually made the abolition of slavery nationwide. It just took longer than anyone would have wanted—seventy years or so.

Q: I'm sure you saw that a school board down in Louisiana recently voted to remove the name of George Washington—or the name of any other slaveholder or person who did not have the respect for equal opportunity—from a local school. What is your opinion of that?

A: Well, I think historical understanding should enable us to live with a past that was different from our world. The Founding Fathers weren't better than we are. They were different. But what they did had an effect on us and on the abolition of slavery. I think that's important to understand, even if they themselves did not abolish slavery. Jefferson did write those words, "All men are created equal," which people from the abolitionists up to Martin Luther King have used to further the cause of greater equality.

We should be more humble. There are many things that we're probably doing today that are going to look to be morally suspect two hundred years from now. One has to have a sense that the past is different and can't be easily condemned by a different present.

Q: In your opinion, are historians supposed to follow the flag or not?

A: There was a time when most people thought that history was the inculcation of patriotism. What you have in many cases today is the opposite. There is the kind of—somebody called it the black armband view of history—in which you just go back and lament the dispossessions and the cruelties that have gone on before. And certainly there are enough of those instances to make a great story. But today I think a lot of our writing by professional historians is a kind of great lament over missed opportunities. That we didn't abolish slavery entirely in 1776. That we didn't give women the vote. That we didn't make for equal distribution of wealth.

All of these things have led some historians to think of the American Revolution as a failure. And they've actually used that term, "It failed." You can only remind those people that they're applying present-day standards to a past event. And that doesn't necessarily work.

Q: Would you give us four or five great historical markers in the periods both prior to the Revolution and during it?

A: Of course, the crucial event at the beginning is the Stamp Act, which galvanized the colonists, made them realize for the first time that the British empire could be hostile to their interests. And then there are a series of events that led up to the Revolution. But if you're looking for the really important markers, then the Declaration of Independence is the great event in our history. This was when we became the United States of America.

The next marker would be the formation of the Constitution. And then, I think, Washington's first term as president. Those would be crucial points. Then there was Jefferson's election—he himself thought that was more important than the Revolution itself.

Q: Did he really?

A: Yes. Because he felt that the country was going down a monarchical path, a restoration of monarchy. That's how serious the turmoil was in the 1790s. It would have been the end of the republican experiment. So he felt that he saved the United States from monarchy. In his own mind, his revolution became as important as the original one.

Q: You don't believe that, do you?

A: I don't think the Federalists' threat of monarchy

was as great as Jefferson thought it was. And the social forces were such that there was no way that they could have imposed monarchy on the country. Nonetheless, Jefferson's election became a kind of ratification of the democratic social process.

Q: You didn't mention the war itself.

A: The war itself, of course, was crucial. We had to win the war before we could become independent. And I'm sure historians would argue about this. If it hadn't been for French intervention, would we have won? I think it would have been difficult for the British to conquer us, but the Americans' will to resist might have collapsed, and it might have gone on in guerrilla warfare. Who knows? Washington never really contemplated that kind of guerrilla warfare, but what would have happened if he hadn't won at Yorktown?

The country was coming apart. The morale was terribly low. There were mutinies in the army. It was a tough situation there. But I really think that it was almost impossible for the British to recover their empire here. They would have had to have bayonets at every door. And in the eighteenth century, they weren't capable of that kind of totalitarian control. So, to one extent or another, I think the country would have gradually become free if we hadn't won at Yorktown.

Q: Can you give me the most cogent reason there is for us, at the close of the twentieth century, to understand that period of our creation back two hundred years ago?

A: Historical knowledge is essential for understanding yourself in the present. It's like an individual without memory. A person suffering from amnesia is a scary, lost person. And a society that doesn't understand its past, and doesn't understand it correctly, is going to make all kinds of mistakes in the present.

I don't think there are particular lessons to be learned from any particular event in the past. But what the past does teach you is wisdom—the sense of being part of a larger process. There are circumstances, cultural traditions, histories that impinge on you and prevent you from doing certain things. To be aware of those conditions, to be aware of those circumstances, is important for decision makers in the present. They've got to know and we as a public have got to know what our past was like if we're going to be functioning citizens in the present.

CHAPTER TWO

James McPherson
on the Civil War
and Reconstruction

James McPherson, one of the foremost experts on the Civil War, came to his passion partly through pedigree—his great-grandfather and his great-great-grandfather fought in that conflict. But McPherson developed a deeper interest in the war during the 1960s when he began delving into issues surrounding slavery, a study that eventually flourished into the twelve books he has written about the Civil War era.

His history of the war, *Battle Cry of Freedom,* won him the Pulitzer Prize and became a national bestseller. In an attempt to discover the deepest motives that animated the soldiers on both sides, he pored through thousands of contemporary letters and diaries to write *What They Fought For* and his latest book, *For Cause and Comrades.* Recently, he edited the revised edition of the *American Heritage New History of the Civil War.*

McPherson is the George Henry Davis Professor of American History at Princeton University, where he has taught since 1962.

Q: You grew up in the northern plains. In North Dakota?

A: I was born in North Dakota. I grew up in Minnesota.

Q: And was the Civil War a big thing when you were growing up?

A: No, my interest in the Civil War really dates from my graduate-school years at Johns Hopkins in Baltimore, which is much closer to the Civil War. It was close in a particular kind of way when I was a graduate student there, in the late 1950s and the early 1960s. At the time, Baltimore was in many ways a southern community. It was largely segregated. Although the schools had been desegregated immediately after the *Brown* decision, restaurants, hotels, and other public facilities still were very much southern. And while I was there, the civil rights movement was reaching kind of a climax with the freedom rides in '61, the Meredith controversy at the University of Mississippi in 1962.

I was suddenly struck by the parallels between the time in which I was living—with confrontation between the national government and southern governors who vowed massive resistance to federal law, federal troops being sent into the South, violence over the issues of race and race relations. There was a kind of déjà vu quality to this because I knew enough about American history to know that these issues had been the source of sectional conflict in the Civil War, exactly a hundred years earlier. Martin Luther King was pressing President Kennedy to issue a new Emancipation

Proclamation on the hundredth anniversary of the original.

And so I got very much into history because of my contemporary world and the issues that surrounded me in that contemporary world. So I did my doctoral dissertation on the abolitionists, both black and white, people I described as the civil rights activists at that time. During and after the Civil War, they pressed for civil rights, political rights, education for the freed slaves, in rhetoric that in many ways was similar to the kind of rhetoric that surrounded me in the early 1960s. So that was my entrée into the Civil War, and it's expanded into other aspects ever since.

Q: The civil rights movement of the nineteenth century was led by white abolitionists and the civil rights movement of the 1960s was led by blacks, was it not?

A: As a generalization, that's right. But there were a lot of black abolitionists as well. Some of them are not very well known, but some are very well known. Frederick Douglass became the principal one. It was an interracial movement. Of course, like the modern civil rights movement, there were tensions between black and white leaders in the abolitionist movement. But for the most part, they saw eye to eye ideologically. They were egalitarians in a society that was predominantly racist, and they had to challenge the mores in both North and South. And they certainly faced more resistance than the civil rights activists of the 1960s.

But of course in the 1960s, we had northern college students, mostly white, going south to participate in Freedom Summer. And so there was an interracial aspect to the 1960s as well.

Q: What is it that remains so bewitching about the Civil War?

A: The Civil War, in many different dimensions, was the most important and powerful single event in American history. Now that's saying a lot, because it means that it was more important, more powerful, in shaping this nation than the Revolution itself, which gave birth to the nation. But the Revolution of 1776 had left two big questions unresolved, and the Civil War resolved both of them. Those two big questions were, first, Would this republic survive in a world in which most nations were monarchies or some other kind of nonrepublic status? In other words, could a democratic society hold itself together?

The lessons of history at that time were not very encouraging. Most republics up to that time had gone down the tube. They had collapsed in internal civil war or had succumbed to dictatorship. And, indeed, some Americans alive in the 1850s had seen two French republics rise and fall, in their own lifetimes. And so the survival of a republican nation as a single nation was very much unresolved. There was an obsession among Americans about whether their nation really would survive or would fall apart and succumb to despotism as so many republics through history had done. The Civil War really resolved that question. It was a great test, as Lincoln said at Gettysburg, whether a nation conceived in liberty could survive or would perish from the earth.

The other unresolved question left from the Revolution was the institution of slavery. It had been abolished in the states north of the Mason-Dixon line during or after the Revolution. But it had become further entrenched in the states south of that, with the cotton boom of the nineteenth century. And here was a country

founded on a charter that declared all men created
equal with an equal right to liberty that had become, by
the 1830s and '40s, the largest slaveholding nation in
the world. As Lincoln put it, "this monstrous injustice of
slavery" undermined our professions of liberty and
made other nations say with plausibility that we were
hypocrites.

Well, the Civil War resolved that question by abol-
ishing slavery. It also reshaped the nation and reshaped
its development. In the antebellum generation, there
was really a contest between two visions of the direction in which the United States should develop. Would
it become an agrarian, decentralized society dominated
by plantation agriculture, or would it move in the direction of commercial and industrial development, urban-
ization? That contest, while not entirely settled by the
Civil War, nevertheless assured that the future of American development would be in the direction of a commercial, industrial, and rapidly urbanizing society.

One can envision an alternative to what we now
look back upon as inevitable in the course of American
development: What if the Confederate states had
succeeded in establishing their independence? The
North would have developed in that industrial direction, but nobody can say for sure what direction the
South would have developed in. So in all these ways, I
think the Civil War really was crucial in shaping American development.

Then there's one other factor that helps to explain
why it continues to fascinate us. And that is simply the
huge cost, the dramatic scale. Six hundred thousand
soldiers at least, probably more than that, lost their
lives in that war. That was 2 percent of the American
population of 1861. If 2 percent of the Americans were
today to lose their lives in a war fought by this country,

the number of American war dead would be 5 million. So you can imagine the kind of demographic and psychological and cultural shadow that something like that experience casts down the generations, even today, five generations later.

Q: Do you think southerners will ever get out from under the legacy or the burden of the Civil War?

A: There's a paradox about the legacy and the burden of the Civil War in the South. On the one hand, southerners through most of the twentieth century, I believe, have been the most nationalistic and patriotic of Americans, the most willing to support the American flag. A higher percentage of southerners than people from other parts of the country enlist in the United States armed forces. Southerners in Congress tend to support nationalistic and patriotic causes more than people from other parts of the country. And that's a real irony. Because for a generation after the Civil War, southerners still had difficulty in waving the American flag and pledging allegiance to the United States. After all, they had given so much to try to separate themselves from the United States. So in that sense, yes, they have gotten out from under the burden of the American Civil War. But in other respects, either it took a very long time for them to get out or they have not yet gotten out.

For example, it took them a very long time to get out from under the economic impact of the war on the South. Basically, the Civil War destroyed the southern economy, which had been based on plantation agriculture. That never really recovered. And until the 1940s, or even 1950s, the South—as Franklin Delano Roosevelt had said in the 1930s—was the nation's number one economic problem. It lagged in all kinds of economic, educational, and social indicators. And to a considerable extent, that was the legacy of the Civil War.

In terms of race relations, even though the war abolished slavery and the constitutional amendments that grew out of the war established racial equality—on paper, anyway—there was bitterness. The determination of southern whites to salvage at least something from the wreckage of their attempt to establish an independent nation based on slavery resulted in a system of Jim Crow in the South, which persisted until the 1960s. And that, too, I think, was a legacy.

In both the economic and racial relations areas, I think the South has largely—not entirely, but largely—emerged from that burden in the last thirty or forty years. But in another respect—we might call it psychological—there is still a burden, a legacy of the Civil War. With a lot of southern whites whose ancestors fought in the war, or even if their biological ancestor didn't fight in the war, there's a tendency to identify with the generation that fought in the war. They identify with the underdog, with those who fought the good fight against difficult odds, who almost won.

The Confederate leaders have a kind of mythic status in the South. Robert E. Lee, Stonewall Jackson, and the rest of them are enshrined in bronze or granite in virtually every southern community of any size across the South. Or there's the generic Confederate soldier who stands in the courthouse square. There's a kind of symbolic identity with the generation of the Confederacy, which southerners still live with. I think it's a matter of pride to them. But it's also a source of divisiveness because of well-known controversies that are ongoing in the South about the Confederate flag, about the song

"Dixie," the symbolism of the flag, what does it mean. In that respect, they have not escaped from the legacy of the Civil War, and I think it will be a long time before they do, if ever.

Q: You know that passage in Faulkner's *Intruder in the Dust*: There is a moment on a July afternoon when every fourteen-year-old southern boy looks up the slopes at Gettysburg and says, "Maybe this time"?

A: Maybe this time we'll punch through and win our independence. Yes. That's a passage that I have often quoted to illustrate the very point we're talking about.

Q: But, today, going through the South and seeing Richmond and Atlanta and Birmingham and New Orleans with new money and a burgeoning middle class, it seems that the South no longer lives in the past. It's a totally different part of the country now, isn't it?

A: You're quite right in all of the respects that I mentioned a few moments ago: in politics, in nationalism, in the economy, in race relations, even in the spirit of looking toward the future rather than lingering in the past. But just think back a year or so to the controversy over putting a statue of Arthur Ashe on Monument Avenue in Richmond. It divided the city. And most whites, at least initially, did not want to do so because Monument Avenue is where they celebrate their Confederate heroes.

It was a divisive issue because the black segment of the Richmond community was also looking to the past, and they were seeing these symbols of Confederate heroes as symbols of slavery and oppression. And they wanted Arthur Ashe there as a way of saying we need to move beyond that. Monument Avenue is a monument to the present and the future, and to the black community as well as the white and Confederate community. But there were a lot of people in Richmond and in other parts of the South who found that difficult to swallow.

And the same kind of controversy exists with respect to the Confederate flag in South Carolina or Georgia. So despite the Sunbelt prosperity of cities like Atlanta and Dallas and Birmingham and so on, there is this other side, which is a kind of nostalgia. Think of the popularity that persists for a movie, or book, like *Gone With the Wind*.

Q: Or the popularity of the Ken Burns series on the Civil War. How do you account for that?

A: I account for that in many of the same ways that I accounted earlier for the fascination with the Civil War. But there are a couple of other dimensions in the case of the popularity of the Ken Burns documentary. It was emotional. People identified with it emotionally, partly through the music, but most of all through the conjunction of these sepia-tone photographs of Civil War figures with the words that they had written in their diaries or in their letters. And that brought everything to life for millions of the viewers, and demonstrated that here was a generation of human beings just like us who went through this horrific but also powerful and meaningful experience. And it came to life for them, and they were able to identify with the emotions of this.

I think that helps to explain the persistent popularity of the Civil War. Ken Burns was able to dramatize it more successfully than anybody else. But one of the things I've done in my research in recent years is to read thousands and thousands of soldiers' letters from the Civil War, both Union and Confederate, in an attempt to explain what made them tick and to explain why they fought. And I can identify emotionally with the fears, aspirations, and loves and hates of these people as I read them on the printed page. No other generation of Americans, except possibly the generation that founded the country in 1776, has gone through that kind of experience.

Q: It's also true that those armies that fought back then were among the most literate generation in our history. I mean, they certainly weren't as literate in World Wars I and II were they?

A: No. In the years between the Civil War and World War I, a very large number of European immigrants had come to this country from countries with poor educational systems. And so the literacy rate was actually lower for white Americans in the early part of the twentieth century than it had been in the 1860s. By the census definition of literacy, 94 percent of the northern people were literate in 1860, and most of those who were not were recent Irish immigrants. Eighty-three percent of the whites in the South, age ten and older, were literate. So these were the most literate armies—certainly up to that time in history—in any society.

Moreover, there was no censorship of Civil War soldiers' letters as there was in World War I, World War II, Korea. So they could write what they really thought. And that's what gives those letters a kind of poignancy and power and immediacy that I don't think we have for any other historical period.

Q: I read somewhere that you were surprised at the popularity of your book, the *Battle Cry of Freedom*. The copy I have is in its fifth printing. And that's pretty unusual for a fairly massive book to go into that many printings, isn't it? How do you explain that?

A: Actually, the last time I signed hardcover copies of *Battle Cry of Freedom,* it was in the eighth printing. And the paperback was in its eleventh printing. You're quite right, both my publisher and I were surprised by this. I still don't know exactly how to explain it, except that perhaps I caught a rising wave of interest in the Civil War in the late 1980s when I published this book—that same rising wave of interest that made the Ken Burns series so popular. I don't know exactly why that interest began to rise in the 1980s.

One thing I do know, because I lived through the process, is that in [the] late 1960s and [the] 1970s, two things happened that caused interest in the Civil War to plummet to probably the lowest point it had ever been since 1865. One was a kind of reaction of fatigue from the centennial celebration from 1961 to '65, which, in some ways, was kind of a fiasco. And the other was the Vietnam War and the reaction to it. It started with the academic community and increasingly moved to the American population as a whole.

There was a time in the late 1960s and the '70s when nobody wanted to hear anything about wars. American military history was discredited. The number of people applying to the service academies—West Point, Annapolis—declined to one of its lowest levels. Anything to do with the history of war and military history was very unpopular. And, of course, the Civil War caught that in reflection. As we begin to move away from that, and as we begin to see Vietnam veterans as not evil but rather as victims of something that was beyond their control, I think there has been a revival of interest in American military history. And the Civil War benefited from that as people came also increasingly to understand just how important that experience was in molding all Americans.

Q: How close did the South come to winning the Civil War? Did it ever get close?

A: Yes, the South came close to winning the war on several occasions—three in particular. Before I point out what they were, though, I should explain that winning the war for the South meant something quite different, and indeed considerably less ambitious in military terms, than what winning the war had to mean for the North. The Confederacy started the war in complete political and territorial control of all the land that it claimed. That's unusual for a civil war or a revolution. Usually, the rebellious or insurrectionist or revolutionary movement has to fight to gain control of the government or territory or both. The Confederacy already had

that. So to win the war for them meant merely to prevent the enemy from invading, conquering, occupying,
and defeating and destroying the defensive forces to
maintain the control of that territory. To win the war,
the North had to do all those things if they'd conquer,
occupy, and destroy the will to resist.

Given that, there were several occasions when the
Confederacy came close to winning. The first major such
occasion was in the fall of 1862, when not only did they
manage to maintain control of the territory they had to
control, but they sent two invading armies into Maryland and Kentucky to try to win those border slave
states for the Confederacy. If the invading army in Maryland, in particular, Robert E. Lee's Army of Northern
Virginia, had succeeded in winning another battle, coming on top of several other battles that Lee had won in
Virginia that summer, one thing for sure would have
happened—the British and French would have offered
diplomatic recognition of the Confederacy as an independent nation among nations. We know this from the
correspondence of the foreign ministers and prime ministers of Britain and of France.

Furthermore, if Lee had won another battle, there
would have been a Democratic victory in the fall con-
gressional elections in the North in 1862. This would
have discredited the Lincoln administration's war policies. And it probably would have given ascendance to
the so-called Copperhead, or Peace Democratic Faction,
in the Democratic Party, which wanted a negotiated
peace. That would have been tantamount to recognizing
Confederate victory.

Well, as it turned out, in drawn tactical battles at
Antietam and Perryville in September and October of
1862, those two Confederate efforts failed, and those
two Confederate armies had to retreat back to Virginia

and Tennessee. But they had come mighty close. And again, when Lee invaded Pennsylvania in the summer of 1863, it came as a result of another series of Confederate victories at Fredricksburg and Chancellorsville. This was also the frustration of Grant's efforts to capture Vicksburg. The Confederacy again seemed to be on a roll, and the Lincoln administration's policies of preserving this union by military victory and by destroying the Southern will to resist seemed to be a failure.

Well, again, it was a near thing. But the Union forces turned back Lee at Gettysburg, and of course, Grant, a day later, managed to capture Vicksburg. That is often regarded as the major turning point in the war. Some say that after that, the Confederacy had no chance to win. But that's not quite true. In the spring of 1864, there was great hope in the North that the dual offensives being launched by Grant in Virginia and Sherman in Georgia would bring this war to an end by the fourth of July. The Confederacy seemed to be on the ropes. But after three months—May, June, and July 1864—with terrible casualties suffered especially by the Army of the Potomac in Virginia, the Northern people were becoming exceedingly discouraged. War weariness was creeping over the North like a pall. There was a rising peace sentiment.

Again, the peace wing of the Democratic Party looked like they probably would dominate the Democratic convention. And, indeed, for the most part, they did. They wrote a peace plank in the platform saying [that] after four years of failure to restore this store by war, it's time to declare an armistice and negotiate with the Confederacy. Of course, they said negotiation would bring the South back into the Union, but nobody believed that.

Lincoln wrote a famous blind memorandum in

August 1864 saying that he was likely to lose the election. And that would have been seen as a repudiation of the attempt to restore the Union by military victory. Again, it was a near thing. But Sherman's capture of Atlanta on September 2, and a series of Union military victories in the Shenandoah Valley of Virginia, radically transformed the situation. Lincoln now was triumphantly reelected as the commander in chief of a victorious army rather than the failed commander of a defeated army. And after Lincoln's reelection in November 1864, the Confederacy had no chance.

But up until the events that preceded and made possible that reelection, there was a real chance that the North would just give up—just as the United States finally decided to throw in the towel and negotiate a peace with Vietnam in 1972 and 1973. And of course, we say that the North Vietnamese won that war because the United States gave up and pulled out. If the United States—or the Union—had given up and pulled out, as looked very possible in the late summer of 1864, the Confederacy would have won that war.

So on three separate occasions, under different kinds of circumstances, but with a lot of similarities, the Confederacy came quite close. And it was only because of the fortunes of the battlefield and the strategic and tactical developments of those campaigns and those battles that it did not happen. But it might have happened. There was nothing inevitable, in other words, about Union victory in the Civil War. I don't agree with Shelby Foote, who has said that the South never had a chance to win that war. He feels that the North fought the war with one hand behind its back; if necessary, it would have just brought out that other hand and smashed the South.

You could say the same thing about the United

States in Vietnam. In a way, a lot of people have said that we fought that war with one hand behind our back. But it was never politically possible to bring out that other hand and make this an all-out, total war. The American electorate wouldn't have supported that. And I think the Northern electorate wouldn't have supported that either, without those victories in September and October 1864 that made Lincoln's reelection possible.

Q: So what made the difference? It was not necessarily numbers, because smaller armies have defeated bigger armies. It wasn't the loss of will, was it?

A: In the end, I think it was the loss of will. By the spring of 1865, the Confederates had lost the will to continue on because they had been so badly beaten. I mean, they just didn't have the means to carry on, except in guerrilla warfare. There is a school of thought that says the Confederacy could have continued to fight if they had scattered to the bush and fought a guerrilla warfare like Castro in Cuba, for example, or like the Chechens in Chechnya in these last couple of years. That, to me, is not very persuasive. I think the social structure of the Confederacy, its leadership, made it impossible for them to fight the kind of guerrilla warfare that other revolutionary movements have fought at other times.

So I would say that after Lincoln's reelection, and especially in the spring of 1865, the Confederacy lost the will to continue fighting. It wasn't inferior numbers; you're absolutely right. Because the United States won its independence in 1783 against the most powerful navy and one of the most powerful armies in the world with a tiny country of 2 to 3 million people. I think there's a complex series of reasons why the North won. Part of it has to do with Lincoln's leadership, both his political leadership and his leadership as a commander in chief.

It has to do with the dogged persistence of the Northern people. Although they came close to throwing in the towel on one or two occasions, as I've just described, they never did. They did continue to support this war through four years. They supported it despite larger casualties than any other army, except the Confederate army, has suffered in American history. It has to do with the eventual emergence of talented, determined military leadership in the North: Grant, Sherman, Sheridan, Thomas. It took a long time for those four men to emerge as the architects and leaders of Northern military policy.

One of the reasons that the Confederates came so close to winning earlier is because of the incompetence, mistakes, and wrong kinds of strategy on the part of the Northern military leadership. There's another dimension to this as well. In the first part of the war, the Northern goal was to restore the Union. Restoration—that's a conservative goal. We want to restore this country the way it was in 1861. But of course, in 1861 the nation had slavery.

By 1863, Lincoln and a majority of the Northern people had made the decision that we were not going to restore this nation the way it was in 1861. We were going to destroy the slave power that the Northerners thought brought on this war. We were going to destroy the backbone of the Confederacy, of the Southern economy that supported the Confederacy—slavery. And we were going to give this nation a new birth of freedom. It took a while for the Northern people to come around to that really radical, even revolutionary, policy of destroying the social structure of the South and destroying the basic economic institution that underlay that social structure of the South.

They also enlisted nearly 200,000 blacks to fight on the side of the North as soldiers and sailors. That was another dimension that made Northern victory possible, but that was not a dimension that got fully into operation until the last year or year and a half of the war.

Q: So then, is the key word leadership?

A: If you had to pick one word that's key, I would say it's leadership.

Q: Compare Abraham Lincoln to Jefferson Davis, and Robert E. Lee to Ulysses S. Grant.

A: Well, in hindsight, of course, we can say that Lincoln was a far better leader than Jefferson Davis. But contemporaries didn't always think so. In fact, they would almost reverse that equation until the very end of the war. Look at the comparative qualifications of the two men as people would have viewed it in 1861 or even 1863. Jefferson Davis had a West Point education. He had commanded a regiment very effectively and heroically in the Mexican War. He had been a very successful secretary of war for four years in the 1850s and done a lot to modernize the American army. He had been a senator for several years as well. He had all of the qualifications of experience, education, and leadership.

Who was Abraham Lincoln? He had the total of one year of schooling, a few weeks at a time in the frontier blab schools of the 1820s—

Q: Blab school? What is that?

A: That's Lincoln's own word. You would repeat from memory—*blab* from memory—what you had read. Or you would recite a multiplication table as a way of learning it. That's why he called them blab schools. He had little political experience; he had served four terms in the Illinois legislature and one term in Congress. He had no military experience at all. He was not regarded as the most able leader of his party when he was elected. And these images persisted through much of the war. It's only in retrospect that we have come to see Lincoln as a far superior leader to Davis.

And I do think he was, partly because of his innate abilities. He had an almost intuitive grasp of the essential requirements of leadership. He understood not to get too far ahead of his own party and of public opinion, but to maneuver in such a way as that he brought public opinion and his party along in the direction that he thought the country ought to go. He was very skilled at doing that, partly through the use of words and partly through the use of negotiations with party leaders like Lyman Trumbull and William H. Seward.

He was a terrible administrator, but he had the ability to delegate administrative responsibilities. So he picked a very talented cabinet. He had Seward as secretary of state. And when he got Edwin M. Stanton in there—the secretary of war was really an effective leader. Other cabinet officials also knew what they were doing. The North had better leadership than the Confederacy in that respect, especially in the secretary of war.

Lincoln knew how to delegate responsibilities, but he also knew how to make the tough decisions. The decision to fire McClellan. The decision to issue the Emancipation Proclamation. The decisions to stick with Grant when everybody else said this guy is a drunkard. Lincoln made those decisions, and once he made them, he stuck with them. He was able to bring along the requisite political support. And he was able to use his party to mobilize support for these things.

Now, the Confederacy had basically suspended party politics for the duration of the war. There were no party politics in the Confederacy. At first glance, that might seem to be an advantage for a political leader like Davis. He didn't have to look over his shoulder at the opposition party. But in fact, it turned out to be a big disadvantage because the existence of an opposition party in the North tended to unite Republicans behind Lincoln's war policies. Sometimes they were even out in front of it.

The absence of an opposition party in the Confederacy meant that opposition to Jefferson Davis, which became increasingly sniping, came from all over, and he had no party that he could mobilize to support his policies. And in fact, the Confederate constitution had departed from the American Constitution by making a single six-year term for the presidency. The president was not eligible for reelection. There was no sense of loyalty to the president because he might be reelected. So Davis was not able to mobilize support through the political structure.

There were other dimensions to this. Davis had extremely thin skin. He had a very fragile ego. He could not tolerate criticism. He tended to think that if people criticized his policies, they were attacking him personally, and he would reply in kind. Lincoln had the thickest of skins, and he separated political opposition and criticism from personal likes or dislikes. For example, Lincoln had more trouble with General McClellan than anybody else probably—both while McClellan was a general and then later, of course, when he ran for president against Lincoln. But while the war was still going on, Lincoln once said, "I'll hold McClellan's horse if he'll only give us victory."

One cannot imagine Jefferson Davis saying that about Joseph Johnston or Pierre Gustave Toutant Beauregard, both of whom he was at odds with. It just wouldn't happen. Furthermore, Lincoln was in relatively good physical health during the whole war. He had a strong physical constitution. He was almost never sick. Jefferson Davis was blind in one eye. He suffered from neuralgia and what in those days was called dyspepsia, probably an ulcer. He was sick much of the time, which of course increased his bad-tempered dislike of critics. And I think that makes a difference.

With respect to Grant and Lee, I think everybody would agree that Lee was probably the best tactical commander of any Civil War army commander. That is, he had the ability—which slipped once, at Gettysburg—to handle troops, to lead troops, to inspire troops on the field of battle. In that sense, he was by far the best among any top commanders in the Civil War.

I think Lee had a somewhat limited strategic vision. Lee was a Virginian. He had not decided to go with the Confederacy until Virginia seceded. Up until that time, he had opposed secession. He led an army that was called the Army of Northern Virginia, and most of the top commanders, corps commanders, and even many of the division commanders in that army were Virginians.

Lee's vision of where the war could be won and might be lost was in Virginia. And as a consequence, he failed to grasp the larger strategic components of the war. The war didn't quite take place just in Virginia. It took place in other areas like Tennessee and Georgia and Mississippi and Arkansas and Louisiana. Because of Lee's prestige and his influence with Jefferson Davis, the Confederacy concentrated too many of its resources in the Army of Northern Virginia and in the fight in Virginia. So while Lee was keeping the front door shut against Union armies through 1862, 1863, and much of 1864, they were flooding in the back door in Tennessee, in Georgia.

Grant, by contrast, started out the war in Illinois, Kentucky, Tennessee, Mississippi, then Georgia before he came to Virginia. So he had a much wider geographical and strategic grasp of the continental nature of this war. In the end, I think that makes Grant the greatest strategist of the war, and this was a war of strategy rather than tactics. It was the ability to destroy the infrastructure of the Confederacy, tear up its railroads, wear down its army's abilities to resist—not through one or two or three spectacular single battlefield victories, but through campaigns that went on for a year, as Grant's campaign in Virginia from the Wilderness to Appomattox did—that won the war. It was not the really flashy and brilliant tactical victories that we associate with Lee, those at Manassas, Chancellorsville, Fredericksburg, and so on.

Q: So after Grant took command of the Union forces, the war changed from a contest of individual battles to a war of attrition?

A: That's quite true. From the spring of 1864 to the spring of 1865, when the war came to an end, the war wasn't fought in terms of individual big battles like Gettysburg, Antietam, Chancellorsville, and so on. After those battles, the armies sort of pulled apart from each other. One army occupied the battlefield and declared victory, the other retreated back across the nearest river. But by mid-1864 the armies were in continuous contact with each other every day, sometimes almost twenty-four hours a day—day after day, month after month, until the end of the war.

The war took on a different character in 1864. It became much more modern. It anticipated World War I. For one thing, it was fought from trenches much of the time. By 1864 both armies were entrenching at every place they stopped. And then for the last ten months of the war, it looked like the western front in World War I, particularly in Sherman's Georgia campaign. Both armies would entrench all the time. That was new. That anticipated the future. And this was a campaign, not a series of battles.

Q: I read somewhere that after the Battle of the Wilderness in 1864, Grant didn't withdraw like most of his predecessors did after losing. And when he didn't withdraw, Robert E. Lee knew he had a problem.

A: Yes, that's exactly right. Exactly a year earlier in virtually the same area, the Wilderness of Virginia, Lee had won a big victory over Hooker at Chancellorsville. And Hooker had retreated across the Rappahannock River. The Battle of Wilderness seemed to have some of the same qualities as the Battle of Chancellorsville. Lee had carried out some successful flank attacks against the Union forces. But instead of pulling back, Grant moved south and Lee knew that he had a problem.

Q: Did the death of Stonewall Jackson in 1863 change the odds measurably?

A: I think it did. Nobody could say for sure how much it changed the odds and in precisely what way, but his absence really affected Lee in the Gettysburg campaign, which came immediately after that. He had to rely on Ewell commanding Jackson's old corps, and Ewell really let him down at Gettysburg in a way that may have made a difference in the outcome of that battle. Most historians of Gettysburg assume that if Jackson had still been alive and had been in command of his old corps, that he would have pressed the attack on the afternoon and evening of that first day—which was a Confederate victory. And that if he had done so, these historians continue, the outcome of that battle might have been quite different. Nobody can say for sure whether that's true, but it might well have been.

Subsequently, Lee missed the mobility and aggressiveness that Jackson had previously provided. Jackson was a kind of striking force. He would strike and hold the enemy, and then Longstreet would come in. It was sort of a left-right punch. Jackson was the left hook, and Longstreet was the uppercut from the right. When Jackson was gone, the left jab was no longer there.

Q: You said that the use of black troops in the Union

army was a critical factor. Was that a factor in the Union victory, or was it just an added benefit?

A: Well, no one can say whether the North would have won the war without the use of black troops, even if it might have taken them a little longer. Lincoln himself said in August 1863, when the experiment was still relatively new, that the heaviest blow yet struck the rebellion was the emancipation and the use of black troops.

And again, in 1864, when he was being pressed to drop emancipation as a condition for peace negotiations, a time when the Northern people were getting discouraged and there was a rising peace movement, Lincoln insisted that he would not drop emancipation. By this time, more than a hundred thousand black troops were fighting for the North. If he betrayed the promise of freedom that he had made with the Emancipation Proclamation, why should they continue to fight for us? And if they didn't continue to fight for us, how could we win this war? So Lincoln clearly thought that it made a difference.

Now, I think the place where it clearly made a difference was in support. Most black troops in the Civil War, as in World War I and World War II, were not used as combat troops but basically as what we would today call support troops. In the Civil War, they garrisoned some of the areas, especially in Tennessee and Mississippi and Louisiana, that had been conquered by Union forces. They guarded supply trains. They guarded supply depots. They guarded the so-called contraband camps—areas where freed slaves had been gathered in the Confederate states—and somebody had to guard them against Confederate guerrilla raids or counterattacks by the Confederates.

The use of black troops for these purposes released a large number of white troops for frontline duty, and that was important. As time went on, many of the commanders of black troops, who were white officers—all of the senior officers of black units in the Civil War and most of the junior officers were white—regarded this rear-area use of their command as being somewhat dishonorable. They fought for a chance to fight, to show what they could do. The best-known example of that is Robert Gould Shaw, who kept pressing his commanders to allow the Fifty-fourth Massachusetts to lead the attack, and finally got his chance in the attack on Fort Wagner in July of 1863 that's been dramatized by the movie *Glory.*

Q: How did they do at Fort Wagner?

A: They did very well. They did not take Fort Wagner, but they fought courageously and lost 50 percent of their strength, including of course Shaw, who was killed. That was an immensely important example of the ability of black troops to fight and their willingness to fight. Up until that time, a lot of Northern whites and a lot of Union officers really weren't sure of whether black troops—who after all were mostly former slaves and therefore had been conditioned to fear the white man—were really willing to fight. The Fifty-fourth proved that they were.

And from that time on, more and more black troops were used as frontline combat troops. So I think it did make a difference. I wouldn't want to go so far as to say that the North couldn't have won the war without recruiting black troops. Nobody can prove that. But I'm pretty sure it would have taken longer.

Q: In the waning days of the war, when manpower was a problem in the South, was there ever any consideration of using blacks in the Confederate army?

A: Yes. That was a great debate that preoccupied the Confederacy in the last six months or so of the war. The first prominent suggestion that the Confederates ought to mobilize this resource of manpower came from General Patrick Cleburne in the Army of Tennessee. He was the best division commander in the Army of Tennessee. And the army had lost so disastrously at Missionary Ridge in Chattanooga in November of 1863, that Cleburne sat down and wrote a memorandum, which he got most of his brigade commanders and some of his regimental commanders to sign. It stated, in effect, that one of the reasons why the Confederacy was having a hard time winning this war, getting European recognition, mobilizing sufficient manpower, was slavery and its refusal to consider the possibility of using black troops. He said we ought to do it. Well, he was ahead of his time. That proposal was squelched. And Cleburne, who was the best division commander in that army, was never promoted above division command. I think that was partly, or mainly, because of this proposal, which went against what the Confederacy thought it stood for.

But by a year later, November, December of 1864, more and more people were saying, "You know, we've scraped the bottom of this manpower barrel and look at all these able-bodied, young male slaves. Other societies, other countries like Brazil have managed to enlist slaves as soldiers, and they fought very well. The North has enlisted these people to fight against us. Why don't we do it?"

Well, there was a lot of opposition to overcome in the South, because the assumption was that if you got these black slaves to fight for you, you would have to promise freedom and maybe their families' freedom. And a lot of Southerners said, "What did we go to war for in the first place except to protect slavery from the threat of this black Republican abolitionist, Abraham Lincoln? Now we're proposing to do it ourselves." Other Southerners said, "Look, what we're fighting for is independence, and we're going to lose. We'll lose both independence and slavery. Why not sacrifice slavery, or at least some of slavery, to try to win our independence?"

By January and February 1865, both Jefferson Davis and Robert E. Lee had become converted to this position. Lee published, or allowed to be published, a couple of letters stating that he thought that the Confederates ought to enlist black troops. And his influence by that time was so great that that swayed just enough votes in the Confederate Congress. So in the middle of March 1865, they passed the so-called Negro Soldier Bill, which provided for the enlistment of up to one hundred thousand slaves, with their masters' consent, to fight for the Confederacy. With the implication, although not the explicit promise, that they would be freed. But of course, they would have to be freed by the states because of the states' rights ideas of the Confederacy. Well, that was of course too late.

Q: The war ended thirty days later.

A: Yes, Appomattox came a month later, and so virtually no black troops fought for the South. Two or three companies here and there had been organized and were drilling, but none of them ever saw action for the Confederacy.

Q: But why on earth would the Confederate leaders think that slaves would want to fight for a government that was dedicated to perpetuating slavery?

A: Well, that's a very good question. Robert E. Lee said, "You know, these people are Southerners. And if we promise them freedom, they will fight for their country just as I am fighting for my country." Abraham Lincoln was quoted as saying, "Well, I wish they would try the experiment." His assumption was that of course they would throw down their arms and come over to the North. It was never tried. There were just enough examples, however, of what we might call loyal slaves, or what Southern slave owners would call loyal slaves, who had supported the Confederacy. A lot of Confederate officers, and even some private soldiers who came from planter families, had brought black slaves—servants—with them to the army, who did their cooking, their laundry—the scut work in the army.

A lot of slaves were used as teamsters, as laborers, as wood choppers, and so on for the Confederate army. Some of these slaves had actually, in the heat of battle, been known to take up arms and fight for the Confederacy, unofficially. We're talking about a few dozen or a few hundred, scattered over time. But there were enough of these examples to lead some Southerners to believe that, yes, these people would fight for our side. I, personally, don't think they would have done so on a large scale if the war had gone long enough for it to be tried. But we'll never know.

Q: Was desertion a problem during the Civil War?

A: Yes, the rate of desertion was very high in the Civil

War—primarily because it was being fought virtually in their backyard, in the case of Southern soldiers particularly. And so it was easy to desert. The language was the same on both sides. People could easily pass. These were volunteer, civilian soldiers who never came under the same kind of thorough regular army discipline that regular army troops did—or that draftees and volunteers would come under in future American wars for that matter. These were highly individualized volunteers, recruited regiments who thought of themselves as civilians temporarily in uniform.

And a lot of them had a tendency to go AWOL whenever they felt like it, especially in the South. There was actually no such designation as AWOL during the Civil War, but if you didn't answer roll call, you were carried on the rolls as a deserter. So while the desertion rate was high, much of it, especially in the early part of the war, was what we would today call guys who had gone AWOL. Because they came back.

In the months after Lincoln's reelection, in November 1864, more and more Confederate soldiers said, you know, "Hey, we're losing this war and our families at home are suffering." They were getting letters from their wives saying, "Your kids are starving. Sherman's army is in the backyard and, you know, can't you come home and protect me?" And so the desertion rate really went up for Confederate soldiers.

In some cases, especially at Petersburg, the soldiers themselves were starving because the Confederate supply situation by that time was a disaster. And they knew that if they went over to the Yankees some dark moonless night, all they had to do was say, "Hey, Yank, I'm coming over," that they would get food and shelter and warmth. And so hundreds and hundreds of them were going over to the enemy, almost every night for a while in January and February 1865.

But at times during the war, the desertion rate in the Union army was pretty high also, because of what they regarded as incompetent leadership. This occurred after Fredericksburg especially, a disastrous battle. It was just a useless sacrifice of Union life. A lot of men in the Army of the Potomac, especially if they opposed the Emancipation Proclamation, as did many soldiers who came from Democratic backgrounds, said, "You know, I'm going to bail out of this war." And they did. Sometimes their families would send them civilian clothes in a package—no one was checking packages then—and they'd just take off their uniform and go home.

Q: By Democratic background, do you mean working-class families?

A: They didn't necessarily have to be working class, although they were more likely to be working class than not. They might be from a farm in Pennsylvania and their father might have been a Democrat, and so they believed in McClellan, who had been fired by Lincoln a few months earlier. That really hurt the morale of the Army of the Potomac. And under Burnside, the very next battle was Fredericksburg, which, again, a lot of Union soldiers regarded as a stupid, blundering, useless sacrifice of lives. They said, "You know, this army is no good. The president fired the only commander who knew what he was doing. I'm bailing out."

So there was quite a bit of desertion. But it tends to get magnified if you look at the statistics, where AWOL enters into the statistics as desertion.

Q: Is there a different motive for the Southern soldier compared with the Union soldier for fighting?

A: Well, there was one big difference—the Southern soldiers could legitimately say they were fighting to defend their home and hearth from an invading enemy, because most of the war was fought on Confederate territory and Southern territory. Now, although this motive wasn't forefront in most of their minds, some Southern soldiers could say, "I'm fighting to defend a way of life based on white supremacy and slavery against the threat of these abolitionists who come down here and take our property away and make our daughters marry blacks."

And there was some effort on the part of the Confederate newspapers and leadership to whip up this kind of racial fear among Confederate soldiers. So racial fears and defense of homeland were motives for the Confederate soldiers that, for the most part, didn't exist for Union soldiers. Although, of course, there were some Unionists from east Tennessee, for example, a Unionist area, who were fighting to regain control of their homeland from an invading Confederate enemy. But that was exceptional.

Apart from those two things, I think the motives on both sides were similar. Both of them said that they were fighting to defend the institutions established by the Founding Fathers in the Revolution: self-government, a republican form of government, majority rule, democracy, liberty. All of these great words that were part of the American political language in the nineteenth century, both sides invoked that legacy. And the really tragic irony of the American Civil War is that both sides invoked the same legacy but meant precisely opposite things by it.

Confederate soldiers could say, "I'm fighting for the ideals of 1776. That was the first war of secession against a despotic government. Our ancestors fought for self-government and for the right of majorities in their states to rule themselves, and that's what I'm fighting for."

Northern soldiers could say, "I'm fighting to preserve from ruin and dissolution and destruction that nation founded in 1776. Because if the Confederacy succeeds, this country will go down the tubes. And I'm fighting for majority rule and the Constitution because Lincoln won that election in 1860 by a constitutional majority, and if people start saying, 'Well, we don't like the president, so we'll just bail out, our state will secede,' what will become of the United States? Of course it will be the Disunited States, it will be like Mexico. It will be like South America." That's what Northerners said.

Both of them were invoking these symbols of 1776. And what really impressed me in the research that I did in soldiers' letters was the extent to which they did continue to invoke these symbols of 1776 but were fighting for exactly opposite causes.

Q: When you write about the Civil War, what's more important, what actually happened in the war or what were the causes of the war?

A: I think that most historians are interested in trying to explain causes, consequences, reasons. They're interested in the "why" questions—Why did this happen?— and in some of the "what" questions—What are the consequences? But I am personally convinced that you can't really understand the why questions, the causal questions, unless you understand the actual events. And in fact, events themselves become causes. An event, Lincoln's election as president in 1860, became the cause, or the trigger, the immediate cause for the secession of seven Southern states.

And then the secession of seven Southern states was the cause of a constitutional and political crisis that paralyzed the Northern government and led to the firing on Fort Sumter, which brought on the war. And you can go backward from Lincoln's election and say that was caused by the increasing polarization of the country over the issue of slavery's expansion into the territories, which was the basis for the founding of the Republican Party, and so on and so forth. So you can go both directions from events to discerning causes and consequences in those events. And then those causes help to produce another event.

I see the two as being inextricably related to each other. As an historian, I try to write a narrative of the key events that incorporates my interpretation of the causes, the meaning, and consequences of those events.

Q: But when I read the *Battle Cry*, there's not a lot of stuff about where Rodes's brigade was at four o'clock in the afternoon at Kelly's Ford or whatever. You don't get into that.

A: Well, that book is nine hundred pages long, and if I had gotten into that, it would have been nine thousand pages long. No, I think that it's possible for the lay reader who's interested in the Civil War, even in the military aspects of it, to understand the strategic and even tactical dimensions of a given battle without having to know where Rodes's brigade was and where

Chamberlain's regiment was, and so on. Although in dramatic events, like Chamberlain's regiment at Little Round Top, maybe it is important to know where they were. But not all the time. There is a school of Civil War military historiography that does focus on the nitty-gritty details of battles. And I can read that with enjoyment. But when I'm writing for an audience, most of whom are not going to want to know these things, I try to give them just enough detail to understand the big picture, rather than overwhelm them with a multiplicity of small picture details.

Q: Are you a battlefield buff? I mean, before you write about the Civil War, do you go tramp the battlefield?

A: I have tramped nearly all the Civil War battlefields. Some of them many times. And indeed, before I wrote *Battle Cry of Freedom,* I did go around to all of them. My mode of transportation around the battlefields, where I could do it, was by bicycle. Because you can get a feel for the terrain, but also move faster than walking. You can't get a feel for the terrain by driving. So I biked over most of the Civil War battlefields—some of them several times, particularly Gettysburg.

But over the years, I've also taken many groups—my students, alumni groups, local groups—to Civil War battlefields, principally Gettysburg. It's the closest to where I live, and it's also the one that most people want to see.

Q: Have you got a favorite?

A: I would say that my favorite battlefields are Antietam and Shiloh. They were both important battles. And the reason why I think they are my favorites is that of all major Civil War battlefields, they are the closest to the way they were. They have what is called, in the jargon, the greatest integrity. They've been less impinged on by modern civilization. Especially Shiloh, which is away from any town or city.

Q: Shelby Foote says he wouldn't dare write about a battle unless he'd gone to the battlefield. There's something almost transporting about seeing the topography and sensing the air and the atmosphere.

A: I've had that experience, too. I do have that experience every time I go to a Civil War battlefield. It's not only the topography. When people are describing Shiloh, for example, [they] say that they are aware of the ghosts there. There is a kind of emotional empathy with the people who fought and died there that you can't really experience unless you go physically to the place. It's not something that can be rationally explained. It's a kind of psychological bonding that one achieves through the physical presence of actually being there.

The most powerful example of it that I ever saw was back in 1987, when I took students, Princeton undergraduates, to Gettysburg, as I've done many times. And one of them was a young woman who had written her senior thesis with me that year, on Joshua Lawrence Chamberlain, who was the commander of the Twentieth Maine at Little Round Top and the subject of the novel *Killer Angels* and the movie *Gettysburg*. He's now one of the great icons and heroes of Civil War buffs. Anyway, we went in May after the senior thesis had been turned in.

We walked the route that the Fifteenth Alabama had used when it attacked Little Round Top and attacked the Twentieth Maine. And when we got to the Twentieth Maine monument at Little Round Top, she broke down in tears. And so did several other people. The emotional empathy that she experienced, and obviously others did too, really overcame her. And I've seen it happen at other times as well.

Q: Do you agree with Gary Wills's thesis that Lincoln's Gettysburg Address has been more influential for our democracy than the Declaration of Independence?

A: I wouldn't go quite that far. But I think Wills is on to something when he says that Lincoln's Gettysburg Address helped to define the meaning of the Civil War to the United States and to redefine what the war would mean for the future of the United States. Lincoln's address both invoked the past: "Fourscore and seven years ago, our fathers brought forth on this continent a new nation," and now this civil war we're fighting is the great test of whether that nation or "any nation so conceived . . . can long endure" or "shall perish from the earth." And here we are at this battlefield to dedicate the final resting place of those who "gave the last full measure of devotion" so that the nation founded in 1776, now being tested in 1863, can survive into the future. And we must rededicate ourselves to the task of giving this nation "a new birth of freedom."

That of course looks to the future. So here Lincoln used past, present, and future in 272 words. A magnificently compressed but eloquent lesson of history and definition of the future in order to rally people in the present to continue on to victory. I think it is the single most important 272 words in American history. It doesn't so much surpass the Declaration of Independence as it does fulfill it and help to redefine its meaning for the future. And in that sense, I think Wills is right.

Q: Can you think of another presidential address that had its impact?

A: FDR's first inaugural address, I would say, comes pretty close. "The only thing we have to fear is fear itself." Here is an attempt to rally the American people to confront this great crisis of the Depression, which was eating away at the vitals of American society, to mobilize them to work together for future improvement. I think that comes closest to the Gettysburg Address in terms of being a really important presidential address.

Q: With history being revised, constantly revised, broken down into gender studies, gay studies, black studies, labor studies, of new interpretations coming out all the time, why should any of us trust all you historians? I mean, history is history, isn't it?

A: No, history isn't history. There's no way that we can recapture absolutely, literally, what happened in the past. There's just too much of it, and there are multiple witnesses to what happened in the past. Take the analogy of an automobile accident to which there were ten witnesses. All ten of those people are going to tell a different story about what they saw. History consists of the effort by, in this case, the police investigator to make sense out of what those ten different witnesses saw. What is the most plausible explanation of what happened in this automobile accident?

On a larger scale, that's what the historian is trying to do. There are multiple witnesses that we call evidence to what happened in the past, and why it happened, and what it means, and what its consequences were. Historians, like the police officer, have to try to make sense out of these often conflicting explanations. To take just a very small example of what I mean: in almost any set of reports of a particular action in a Civil War battle, you'll get one officer saying, at 10:27 we did this, and another officer describing the same action saying, this took place at 10:14, or somebody else will say it took place at 11:02. There's no agreement.

So what's the historian going to say about when this happened? This is small potatoes, but it's an example of what I'm talking about. Now why should you trust us? Well, if you think that I, as an historian, or any other historian you're reading, is honest, if we exude some aura of honesty and integrity, then you'll have to trust us. You'll have to trust us just as you trust this police officer to make some honest sense out of the conflicting reports he gets about an automobile accident.

CHAPTER THREE

Richard White
on Westward Expansion

A 1995 recipient of a MacArthur Foundation "genius" grant, Richard White is widely regarded as one of the finest historians specializing in the American West. While earning his B.A. from the University of California at Santa Cruz in the late 1960s, he became involved in Indian politics. He wrote his doctoral dissertation at the University of Washington on the environmental history of Island County, Washington. That work, which became his first book—*Land Use, Environment, and Social Change*—earned him the Forest History Society's prize for the best book published in 1979–1980. This was followed by a number of groundbreaking books—among them *The Middle Ground: Indians, Empires and Republics in the Great Lakes Region 1650–1815, It's Your Misfortune and None of My Own,* and *The Organic Machine.* Winner of the prestigious Francis Parkman Prize in 1992, *Middle Ground* was a finalist for the Pulitzer Prize. Currently the Margaret Byrne Professor of History at Stanford University, White was a major consultant—and commentator—for Ken Burns's PBS program *The West.*

Q: How do you define the West, Professor White?

A: I define the West as all the United States west of the Missouri River. It's a political creation, and the boundaries shift over time. In the nineteenth century, when Americans talked about the West, they were talking about a very different place than they talk about in the twentieth century. The West isn't so much a geographical space as it's a political and social space whose boundaries really do shift.

Q: You wrote a book called *It's Your Misfortune and None of My Own*. That's a line from a song, is it not?

A: Yes it is, "Git Along Little Doggies."

Q: Why did you call it that?

A: I called it that because it seems to me that even though it's a song about cows, it has something to do with human beings. There's a social attitude in large parts of the West, in which the fault for any misfortune lies on the person who suffers from it. It's thought to be their problem to sort out. The West has been the seat of many tragedies, as well as many great successes. But there has been a sense that no matter how many different peoples are in the West—and there are very many—what happens to any one group of them tends to be their problem. Their predicament doesn't meet up with a lot of sympathy from other groups, even though you can predict fairly accurately that other groups are soon going to find themselves in the same boat.

Q: The subtitle for the book is *A New History of the American West.* Why is it new?

A: Well, it came out at a time when there was a conflict between new historians of the West and old historians of the West. And the easiest way to boil down the difference between us is that old historians concentrated on the frontier, their whole study was based on the idea of an expanding frontier that moved steadily from East to West. The new historians abandoned the idea of the frontier and looked at the West as a region that was already settled by people before Americans got there. We looked at the West as the scene of an ongoing set of cultural conflicts that comes under American domination. The Americans settled the West in the late nineteenth and early twentieth centuries, but they weren't moving into an empty area, and the people who were there before them did not disappear.

Q: How could it be that the history of the West winds up with the Indian being the savage and the white conqueror being the victim? I mean, that's upside down, isn't it? How did that happen?

A: It's one of the most amazing things in American history, and I took it for granted for years. The key iconic incidents in western history when I was a kid, and even when I was an adult, were the Alamo and Custer's Last Stand. But a few years ago, when I was working on an exhibit on the West at the Newberry Library, it suddenly occurred to me: Wait a minute—what we're celebrating here, the things we identify as critical incidents in western American history, are instances where the Americans were not only defeated, but they died to the last man. And I began to ask, why is it that Americans celebrate defeat in the West when we won? It really was a conquest, an overwhelming conquest, in which everything was on our side—numbers, weapons, technology.

And I think it's because we have this sense of ourselves as a nation that doesn't participate in conquest, that doesn't conquer a place where in fact we hold all the advantages. We have to give a reason for aggression, and the best reason for it is "They attacked us." In our classic stories of the West, we have scenarios in which we were not only attacked, but attacked barbarically, and all we were doing in the end was defending ourselves.

So it makes a sort of cultural sense that the things we celebrate are not our victories, not the times when we in fact killed thousands of people, but the times when we were defeated. That turns our future actions into simply getting revenge for terrible incidents.

Q: And as a result of that, the Alamo and Little Big Horn are major icons in western history?

A: They certainly are. They're major icons in popular American history, and they're places that people visit in the West. But they're never put into a larger context. They always stand alone: "There is the brave, beleaguered band of white men, attacked by nonwhites." And it's not that these things didn't happen. I mean, clearly Custer was killed and the Alamo was taken, but they take place in this wider context which is totally obliterated. These incidents stand alone and they stand for western history.

Q: Do you trace some of that upside-down history to the great Buffalo Bill?

A: Well, Buffalo Bill would be one of the people who would certainly purvey this. I actually think Buffalo Bill was one of the great geniuses of American history, probably the great genius of the nineteenth-century American West.

Q: He was just a showman, wasn't he?

A: Buffalo Bill would never have let you say "just a showman."

Q: Really?

A: Buffalo Bill would have said that what he was—and this is how he always described his Wild West, which he never called the Wild West Show—was an educational experience. He was educating you in the history of the West.

Q: Like a Disney theme park.

A: No, Buffalo Bill would do better than that. What Buffalo Bill would say is that, unlike Disney theme parks where there are people dressed up like Mickey Mouse and Donald Duck, Buffalo Bill was a real person who had been in the wild West. Some of the Lakota who were attacking at Custer's Last Stand in the Wild West Show were the very Lakota who had attacked the real Custer. Buffalo Bill's claim was "These are the actual people. We were there. We're simply reenacting what we did." Buffalo Bill claimed an authenticity that something like Disney or a theme park really can't, and doesn't, claim.

Q: But how did Buffalo Bill get such a hold on the American public?

A: He did it by telling them exactly what they knew already. In any popular culture, what you want to do is work with the material at hand. You can shape it in new ways at least slightly, but you're never going to be able to start out by having people abandon all their premises. And what Buffalo Bill started with was a way that Americans understood this history already. I mean, these were nineteenth-century people who had grown up— much like we did—on stories of Indian attacks, Indian slaughter, Indian massacres, and brave white men and women overcoming hardship to win the land.

What Buffalo Bill did was simply take these beliefs, claim an authenticity—"I was one of the people who did it"—and then reenact it for them in very predictable ways. And so Buffalo Bill played Buffalo Bill, and Lako-tas played what white people thought Lakotas should be. You had Indians imitating themselves, really.

Q: Lakota is an Indian tribe?

A: Lakota is the westernmost group of Sioux.

Q: The whites call them all Sioux?

A: The whites lumped all the Sioux together, but the Lakota were a group of Sioux Indians.

Q: Tell me about Buffalo Bill. What was his background, where did he come from?

A: Buffalo Bill had been a Pony Express rider as a youth, and later he became a buffalo hunter for the railroads. He'd been a scout for the cavalry. He became a showman. And during a large part of his career, he'd alternate between being a showman and taking part in real events in the West.

On one famous occasion in Baltimore, he stopped a play he was in, stepped off the stage, and told them that he was going to join the Seventh Cavalry in the campaign against the Sioux. And he did. He went out West, and by the time he got there, Custer was dead. But he was a scout, I think for the Sixth Cavalry, and he was engaged in a famous duel with Yellow Hand, who was a Cheyenne warrior.

The interesting thing about his story is that it's hard to say where the theater stops and real life begins. And Buffalo Bill was a master at that sort of postmodern West. He knew that he was going to meet Cheyennes or a Sioux, and he dressed up in a showman's outfit. He dressed up in this vaquero outfit with a, with a big wide hat. He had, I think, lace trim along the edge. It was all this sort of black velvet material. Who knows what poor Yellow Hand thought when he saw this guy coming at him.

But in fact, Buffalo Bill did go out, and there was a duel. And Buffalo Bill killed Yellow Hand.

Q: With his pistol?

A: He killed him with a rifle or a pistol, and then he scalped him. It was a first scalp taken for Custer. Having taken the first scalp for Custer, Buffalo Bill immediately left the cavalry, or soon after left the cavalry and went back on stage.

Q: Taking the scalp with him?

A: Taking the scalp with him. Actually, I think they confiscated the scalp in Boston.

Then he put on a play based on his encounter with Yellow Hand. So his actual incident became theater. It was designed to be theater from the very beginning, and all these things mixed up together. And that's how Buffalo Bill's whole life went.

Q: So in other words, Buffalo Bill's show was the great Broadway hit of the nineteenth century?

A: Well, this was pretty low theater. At this time, Buffalo Bill hadn't formed the Wild West show yet, so this was closer to what would become vaudeville. This was Buffalo Bill often drunk on stage. I mean, there were some amazing things: Buffalo Bill trying to get horses on stage when he was himself drunk; Buffalo Bill cutting up poor Captain Jack Crawford who was playing Yellow Hand in one of these things—Buffalo Bill was drunk and had a real knife and just sliced him up. Jack Crawford never went on the stage with Buffalo Bill again.

So there was a lot of low theater that went on in this stuff. But it brought in audiences, and later it became much more polished. These were his pre–Wild West days. Once he organized that, it was quite a show. Parts of it still survive on film.

Q: What kind of crowds would the Wild West show attract?

A: It would draw an amazing crowd from both working-class people and middle-class people—and indeed beyond that. These shows were immensely popular in Europe. Queen Victoria got a command performance when Buffalo Bill toured England. And he was immensely popular in France. These shows were mass entertainment and cut across society in the late nineteenth and early twentieth centuries. In many ways, they were previews of the classic Western.

Q: And in his show, the white man always won?

A: No, the white man didn't always win. The most

famous scene, of course, was a reenactment of Custer's Last Stand, in which Buffalo Bill himself showed up at the end, and there was a big sign that flashed over the theater, which said TOO LATE.

Q: In your book, *The Frontier in American Culture,* you describe Buffalo Bill as one of the two great narrators of western history. Who was the other one?

A: Frederick Jackson Turner.

Q: What was his great thesis?

A: Well, the Turner thesis is very simple. Turner said that what made Americans was the existence of free land in the West, and it was the constant settlement of that free land, the retreat back to nature—back to barbarism almost—and then the recapitulation of progress out of this initial retreat that made Americans who they are. It made them democratic, it made them egalitarian, it made them optimistic. It made them a people who were ready and willing to take advantage of anything that life can put in their way. It also merged a fairly diverse group of immigrants into a single homogeneous group of people.

Q: And who was Frederick Jackson Turner?

A: He was a history professor at the University of

Wisconsin who later moved on to Harvard. But his best days were at the University of Wisconsin.

Q: And did he attract the attention that Buffalo Bill did?

A: He didn't have the same popular attention, of course, but he probably lasted longer in the sense that he framed the way that many Americans look at the world—even if they've never heard of Frederick Jackson Turner. I mean, that's the mark of a great historian: Nobody even knows who you are, but they end up recapitulating most of what you'd said.

Q: Did Frederick Jackson Turner have as much influence as Buffalo Bill?

A: Not immediately, but in the long run, he probably had as much or more. Turner has had the kind of influence that every historian really hopes for, because most people's vision of the West, the one that still is prominent in popular culture today, is Turner's vision. They may never have heard of Turner, but they still look on the West as a land of opportunity, the West that makes Americans into Americans.

Turner did this first by giving what became a very famous paper in 1892, but then he was also something of a self-publicist. He passed out copies of that paper. And by the early twentieth century, it was becoming more and more the dominant way that academic historians viewed the West. It became the explanation of why America was different from Europe.

And this passed into popular culture. It passed into teaching and schools. It passed into books. It passed into politics. It's the kind of thing that shows up in John F. Kennedy's New Frontier, in Ronald Reagan's speeches. It's a version of the West that still has a very powerful life in American popular culture, though it was abandoned by academics.

Q: Why did they abandon it?

A: Largely because it didn't fit the facts of what we knew about the United States. The problem was that relatively few Americans actually moved into the West in the late nineteenth and early twentieth centuries. Most of the American migration wasn't to the West, it was to cities. The West was not more democratic than other parts of the United States. As a matter of fact, democracy came relatively late to the West. In terms of distribution of income or anything else, the West was not more egalitarian than other places in the United States.

And if you look at many of Turner's specific claims, those claims were just wrong. And so those claims undercut the thesis, and academic historians abandoned it. But just because academic historians abandon something doesn't mean that it vanishes from the world. And the Turner thesis continues to live on very strongly in America today.

Q: You yourself said that there was a certain optimism out West that you didn't find matched in the East, so there's some kernel of truth in that thesis, is there not?

A: Well, no, because I'm talking about a twentieth-century optimism. I don't think Turner, even in his wildest dreams, envisioned the Pacific Rim. And the current western optimism has much more to do with events that took place after World War II than anything that Turner had written about.

Q: Was Turner's thesis confined to academia?

A: Initially, it was confined to academia, though he was a very popular lecturer at things like graduations. He talked to many public audiences.

His thesis became widely known mostly because it could be reduced to the sort of capsule formula that's easy to understand: The frontier is what made the United States into the nation it is today. That could be repeated endlessly, over and over and over again. As Teddy Roosevelt said at the time, Turner had managed to bring together many things that had been floating around, which many of us believed, and put them into the form of this frontier thesis. And that's a typical Roosevelt statement, in the sense that he sort of indicated that he himself had been thinking these things but hadn't quite gotten around to putting them down on paper yet. But on the other hand, he's probably right. Turner, like Buffalo Bill, managed to play up things that Americans already believed, but he put them in a more compelling form.

Q: It's almost the equivalent of a thirty-second sound bite, isn't it?

A: Yes, in a lot of ways. Turner's thesis was simple, direct, straightforward, and it made sense in terms of people's experience—if not their actual lived experience, certainly the cultural experience. They had seen these ideas before.

Q: During the period in which western history was being popularized, as you say, the two great narrators were Buffalo Bill and Frederick Jackson Turner. Weren't there any others? Wasn't there another dissenting view, or third version?

A: Not at the time. They had imitators, but they didn't really have competition. Turner dominated academic history really until the 1930s—and even then there wasn't so much a new version of western history as an abandonment of western history as being important to the history of the United States. And Buffalo Bill had plenty of imitators and plenty of rivals, but all they were trying to do was tell Buffalo Bill's story better than Buffalo Bill, and they largely failed to do that. And then Buffalo Bill's Wild West was picked up by the movie western, and it continued on into the twentieth century.

Q: It was folded right into Hollywood.

A: Exactly. In some ways Hollywood would make it much more complex as the century went on, because the advantage of the western is that it's incredibly versatile. If you want to criticize the United States, Indians become good guys; if you want to praise the United States,

Indians become bad guys. So at times when Americans were self-critical, they used westerns to criticize themselves. At times when in fact Americans were pretty satisfied with themselves, they used the western to praise themselves. It's a tremendous cultural vehicle. Buffalo Bill was the first one to really bring it into its full popular form.

Q: What's the best western that was ever made?

A: For me it would be John Ford's *The Searchers*, starring John Wayne. Because it's full of this kind of cultural ambivalence. It has it both ways at once, where you realize—and it's still jarring—that what looked like an attempt to rescue a young woman captured by the Comanches was really Wayne's attempt to kill her, because, as he sees it, she'll never be any good once the Indians have had her. It's a chilling turn in the middle of the narrative that still gives that film incredible power.

Even now, I can show it to classes and there'll be a moment where the students—as jaded as they are—will take their breath in and realize what's happening. It's a very harsh film.

Q: Do you think that history has it about right now— about what the white man did to the red man, and vice versa? Are we in balance now?

A: I don't think we're ever going to be in balance, because we're beginning to recognize that it's a much more complicated story. The older stories are too simple for pretty basic reasons. One of them simply made whites victims of Indians, and the other one turned it around and made Indians victims of whites.

The problem is that there's no real history of Indian people in any of this because in these stories Indians were both savages and victims. There's no sense of these people finding themselves in a very difficult condition and trying to work out a version of the world. Also, in the older stories the history of Indian people essentially ended when their conquest was complete in the late nineteenth century, despite the fact that in much of the western United States, Indian peoples are still very important figures in western politics. In state politics in the last twenty or thirty years, we've seen an incredible resurgence, in many ways, of Indian power.

Q: Is there a unifying approach that the new historians of the West have to the West?

A: Well, the people who are called new western historians and the people who are called the old western historians still agree on far more than they disagree on. The major conflict now is whether you teach the West as a region, the same way southern historians teach southern history, or whether you tell a story of the frontier in which the story starts on the East Coast and steadily marches west.

Q: And does the teaching of the West get broken down into black studies, women studies, ethnic studies, economic studies, social studies, and so forth?

A: I certainly try not to do that.

Q: Why not?

A: Because it seems to me that the interesting thing about American history is not breaking it down into a series of constituent groups and constituent interests with separate stories, but to set up a relationship between this diverse group of people who inhabit the United States, whether the West or any other place. What matters is the relationships between the people, and if you're going to deal with one group at a time, you can't deal with relationships.

Q: Why does the West have so many myths?

A: I think it's not so much that the West has more myths than the rest of the United States, but that the western myths stand for America in a way that myths about other sections don't. The South stands for the South. The East stands for the East as the oldest part, the founding of the United States. But the West stands for the American future. It's the place where America develops, where Americans become Americans. It's the place for whatever the United States is going to be. That's what the western myths have been about. Western myths are for everybody.

Q: You've mentioned the icons of the West—Custer's

Last Stand and the Alamo. Are there other great western icons?

A: Yes, there are other icons that are incredibly important. Turner liked to use the log cabin.

Q: The log cabin?

A: The log cabin, the wagon train—these are things that when you see them now, stories pour out of them. They're used so widely in advertising, political campaigns, and other things. All you do is show the picture of the wagon train, and you know that here's a story of brave migrants setting off into the unknown, taking their destiny in their hands. Where you see a picture of the log cabin, here is somebody setting off in the middle of the wilderness with only their own resources to set up their life, and this is the small beginnings from which great things will flow. Those are icons, those are things that still resonate with meaning for the American people.

Q: Of course, Abe Lincoln was born in the log cabin— and wasn't William Henry Harrison?

A: William Henry Harrison's was actually the first log cabin campaign.

Q: Were they really born in log cabins?

A: Let's see, Abe Lincoln was. William Henry

Harrison—to tell you the truth, I'm not sure. But the important thing for them wasn't that they actually were born in a log cabin—it's that the log cabin means that you start out poor in the United States and you will end up great.

If you're born in a log cabin and you die in a log cabin, it does you no good at all. I mean, who cares about that? What you've got to do is be born in the log cabin but end up in the White House or someplace else. The log cabin is about progress, it's about starting low, but it can only have meaning when you end up high.

Q: So the log cabin became the symbol of man improving himself, carving out of the wilderness something better than a tent or a cave on his way to civilization.

A: Yes, exactly, and remember that it only became a symbol of progress in the nineteenth century. In the eighteenth century, it was a sign of American backwardness. Europeans would comment on these primitive structures Americans lived in, how ugly the countryside was. So Americans took something that had been used to denigrate them and turned it into a sign of progress, "Well, yes, that's where we start; all you're seeing is where we begin, but this is where we're going to end."

Q: Is the twentieth-century equivalent of the log cabin a clapboard bungalow, like one Harry Truman grew up in, or maybe Kennedy's first place?

A: Well, it's hard to see the Kennedys in much of the

log cabin tradition. If you use Kennedys, you have to go back to Ireland and find a thatched cottage or something. But the equivalent you have in the twentieth century is somebody being born into some kind of poverty, at least the lower middle class, and rising up from there.

Americans still don't want leaders who are born rich and end up rich (though in fact that describes most American leaders). Clinton, for example, plays into this sentiment, as somebody who started poor and grew up to be president of the United States. They're still playing to that same story.

Q: So despite the rejection of the Turner thesis by all of you professional historians, it still has a major grip on us, doesn't it?

A: Yes. Turner wasn't inventing this stuff. He simply gave people a version of the way in which they understood their lives already. He didn't invent the log cabin; it was a popular American symbol before that. He just gave it a meaning, not just for personal lives, but for the history of the whole country.

And those symbols remain incredibly powerful. It's one of the things that academic historians have learned with some chagrin—that they're not going to be able to counter myths that have a power beyond fact. These myths have the power of giving people vehicles for making sense of their lives.

Q: What would you say are the major turning points in western history that every schoolchild ought to know?

A: First of all, the acquisition of Louisiana, the Louisiana Purchase, which brought America into the West as a modern state. After that would be the Mexican War, in which the United States conquered another huge swath of the West from Mexico. And then to make the West modern, there are three other points. The first of them is the building of the railroads. The West is impossible without the railroads. After that, I would say the creation of irrigation schemes by the federal government in the early twentieth century. And the final turning point, and in some ways the most important, is World War II. World War II utterly transformed the West—it made the West into the modern section it is today.

During the Second World War, the federal government poured men, materials, and capital into the West on a scale that westerners had only dreamed about before. And because of the Cold War, they maintained that level of spending and development. So the great growth of the West, the growth of western cities, the setting up of the western defense industry, the setting up of western research institutions and the western military bases on which the West has depended for so long—all these things grew out of World War II. World War II was a transformative moment. It really changed the whole place.

Q: The government's policy toward the Indian doesn't figure in to your turning points?

A: Well, the Indian peoples in the West had been weakened by disease before the Americans got there in large numbers, and I'd argue that their ability to resist the American state was less of a force west of the Mississippi than it had been east of the Mississippi. East of the Mississippi, for long periods of time, Indian peoples had real power in their ability to call on European powers as allies.

By the time we got to the western United States, the great disadvantage of the Indians was not only their loss of numbers but their lack of European allies. There was no other European power that they could ally themselves with to play off against the United States. The Indian peoples were on their own. And, furthermore, the Indians were never united; they were fighting us group by group.

In a real sense, they never have a chance. There were victories. The Indians never had problems winning victories against the American army, but they were not going to win wars; they couldn't fight against an industrial state.

Q: So there never was a point, post–Civil War, when the Indians were on the verge of victory?

A: Post–Civil War, I'd say no. There were plenty of places where they defeated American armies, and it certainly was very difficult for American soldiers to subdue them, but there was no point where the real outcome was ever in doubt. The cost the United States was willing to pay, how long it was going to take, how bloody it was going to be—all those things were unclear—but the eventual outcome was certain.

Now, east of the Mississippi, the outcome *was* in doubt. When Indian peoples in the Northwest allied themselves with the French, or the New England Indians allied themselves with the French, they were a powerful barrier, first to the English colonies and later on to the young American government. When Tecumseh tried to unite Indian peoples, North and South, and bring them into alliance with the British, that was a major threat to the United States. But there was no equivalent to any of that west of the Mississippi following the Civil War.

Q: As uncomfortable as our Indian policy may make us today, did the United States really have any choice in the matter?

A: The United States always had a choice.

Q: Could they have just left it to the Indians?

A: No. What they could have done was, in fact, what Indian peoples often wanted to do. Indian peoples were willing to negotiate. Indian leaders realized accommodations were going to be made with European powers, and that indeed there were things to be gained. But did it have to go as far as it did? First of all, we have to remember how far it actually did go. Vine Deloria has said that when you look at American Indian policy and compare it with other policies toward indigenous peoples, the American policy doesn't come out all that bad, despite the horrors that were inflicted on Indian peoples.

The reason is that the United States had always recognized Indians as sovereign nations, or semisovereign nations. We still negotiated with them; they still had rights that could not be wiped out without invalidating treaties. The question then became, Once you recognized them as semisovereign nations, how could they be allowed to develop? Other avenues are apparent. There had always been alternatives, and in hindsight, there might have been better alternatives.

Q: I've never understood how eastern America conquered western America so easily. I mean, compared to the European conquest, which would go through a thirty-year war, and the tearing of the government and the social fabric, our western conquest was fairly easy, wasn't it?

A: It was easy and it was rapid. But I think it had to do with a series of things that Americans often ignore. Again, we forget that on this continent the Indian population was devastated by disease. By the time Americans came to the far West, Indian peoples had been terrifically reduced by smallpox, measles, and other diseases. In some areas they left only 10 percent of the people who had been there before, and in other areas 30 to 50 percent. So these were people who were already in real trouble when they confront Americans.

Q: This was disease brought by white people?

A: By Europeans. These were diseases that came from Europe, and which Indians had no resistance to. These had been playing out for centuries, but the big epidemics really hit the far West in the late eighteenth, early nineteenth century, and preceded American settlement. So the Americans faced an Indian population that, in fact, had already been reduced by disease.

The second point is that by the time the United States reached the far West, it was an industrial nation. We could move through the West so quickly. It took Europeans and Americans a couple of centuries to reach the Mississippi, but after that, it took a generation to really conquer the rest of the West. We forget that they were doing it with things like the railroads. It was an industrial society penetrating this region, and it moved incredibly quickly with modern armies, modern weapons, modern technology.

Finally, it wasn't just an American population moving into the West; there were people moving in from all over the world. It was a massive world migration into the western United States in the late nineteenth and early twentieth centuries. Europeans, Mexicans, Chinese, and Americans were all pouring into the region.

So it was settled with incredible rapidity. It was as if a clock was ticking very, very slowly at the beginning of American expansion, but the dial was just reeling around the clock by the end.

Q: And in our conquest of the West, there were five or six different empires with different languages and cultures—Texas, New Mexico, California, Oregon, and so forth. How did they assimilate all that so easily?

A: Well, the other countries and empires that claimed the West—all before the United States got there—had an incredibly loose hold on it, and they didn't value it as much as they should have, in hindsight.

The British were outnegotiated by the Americans. In the area around Seattle, there were no American settlers—it had not been explored by Americans. And yet the American diplomats succeeded in wresting it away from the British. Mexico was in the throes of its own domestic problems, which made it virtually impossible for it to hold on to its northern provinces, which were taken away by the United States. Before that, the Spanish empire had been incredibly weak. And the Louisiana Purchase was basically a fire sale by the French. They thought that they were going to lose it to the British, and so they sold it, and the United States was able and willing to buy. So there were not strong holds in this region by other powers.

Q: Did we outwit Russia at any point in the West?

A: Well, we outnegotiated Russia, too. Russia had some claims all the way down to California and certainly in Alaska. In hindsight, Russia probably would have been better off keeping Alaska, but they sold it. In all of these instances, the United States moved into a region that was undervalued by the European empire that held it. And in the cases where it was valued—Mexico certainly valued its northern provinces—the power was in such a weakened state that it was incapable of standing up to what amounted to American aggression.

Q: What was the importance of the western artists, like Frederic Remington and Charlie Russell? They were instrumental in keeping the myth alive, weren't they?

A: What Remington and Russell did was enable Americans to visualize ideas that they already held about the West. In terms of Remington, if you wanted to see the West in racial terms, as many nineteenth-century Americans did, you saw Anglo-Saxons moving against people they thought of as inferior. Remington basically showed you that.

Remington portrayed this sort of rugged West of cavalrymen and cowboys, showing the dominant American individualism in action. What's interesting about Remington's work is that actually many of his cavalrymen are black. And in Remington's magazine sketches, he'd show African American cavalrymen. But when he turned them into these monumental pictures of the West, he'd often take the same scene and lighten all the figures so that what had been black cavalrymen in the original sketch become white cavalrymen in a later painting because the paintings went toward the myth.

Russell was more complicated. Russell was not anti-Indian. As a matter of fact, he was incredibly romantic about the Indians. So once Indians were conquered, he took this incredible romantic past, which we now miss, and worked with two figures who immediately became enveloped in nostalgia—the cowboys and the Indians. In Russell's view, both of them were gone, and he portrayed them in this romantic past that supposedly made us who we are. And so Russell played to this sense of nostalgia in the early twentieth century.

Q: I read somewhere that in Remington's painting of Lewis and Clark meeting the Flathead Indians, there was a historical inaccuracy, that he had Indians dressed in cloth, and there was no record anywhere in the Lewis and Clark journals that Indians ever wore cloth at that time.

A: Well, they were probably the Shoshone Indians, and they didn't have cloth. But most Indians did. Remember, by the time Lewis and Clark went through, there was only a small section of the West where Indians hadn't seen Europeans before. After all, when Lewis and Clark reached the Mandan villagers, there were French traders there. In fact, there had been French traders there for almost a century. There had been ships trading at the mouth of the Columbia River since the 1790s, and Lewis and Clark began to see people who were wearing American clothes which had been traded upstream from the Columbia.

But Remington's paintings aren't always historically exact. The power of a painting is never going to be that it re-creates the scene exactly. The power of the painting is that it plays into our vision of what this scene should have been, and Remington had a terrific eye for what nineteenth-century Americans wanted to see.

Q: Despite the western antipathy to the government, the federal government still owns great tracts of land in Wyoming and Utah, doesn't it?

A: That's one of the ways you know you're in the West. As you move into the West, particularly past the Great Plains, you find that large parts of western states are really federal lands, and there's no equivalent to that in the East or the Midwest or the South. The West today is still largely a holding of the federal government. The vast majority of land in states like Nevada are federal lands.

Q: Looking back over presidential history as it relates to the West, who were some of the outstanding presidents who had a feeling for the West and saw it through to policy?

A: You mean people who had a feeling for the West in the sense that they imagined what the West could be? Well, clearly, James K. Polk, whatever his limitations, was the president who made much of the western part of the United States. Polk was responsible for two things. First of all, he was responsible for the annexation of what's now the Northwest—Oregon, Washington, and Idaho—which came in from Great Britain. And secondly, he was responsible for the Mexican War. He very much wanted to acquire territory from Mexico, and he was willing to go to war to do it. He would have preferred not go to war, but he ended up going to war to acquire the Mexican cession, including all of California. He added a huge swatch to the United States.

Without Polk, you might say the United States would have acquired some of it anyway, but it's hard to say we would have acquired all of it, because these boundaries shift back and forth. The boundaries ended up being pretty contingent and arbitrary, and you have to look at Polk and the events of the Polk administration to see where they came from.

Q: And yet, any time historians rate American presidents, Polk ranks quite low.

A: Well, he wasn't a great president. Just because he managed to acquire huge swaths of territory over sometimes large opposition doesn't mean he was a great president. But he was an important president. You can't understand this acquisition without him.

Q: How about Teddy Roosevelt?

A: Teddy Roosevelt was an important president for a couple of reasons. First of all, he reimagined himself as a westerner. Roosevelt played to the western myth. He was the eastern dude who went West and became a westerner and later became the cowboy president. So on a mythological level, he identified with the West. But more importantly, as a progressive president, and he was able to greatly increase the scale at which the federal government managed the West. Whether it was through Gifford Pinchot and the forest service, or irrigation programs, Roosevelt really made the federal government a hands-on manager in the West. That had never been the case before.

The third president who mattered for the West, and probably was the most important, has got to be Franklin Delano Roosevelt. What Roosevelt did, both during the Depression and World War II, was really open up the pipe so that federal money flowed into the West to build up the western infrastructure that was going to make future western development possible. It was Franklin Roosevelt who created the hydroelectric system, expanded the irrigation system, set up the military bases. He was the president who set in motion events in the West that carry down to the present day.

Q: Is there one president who deserves credit for

the development of the national park system in the West?

A: There's no single president who can claim that. The national park system came incrementally, in pieces. And the notion of what national parks are supposed to be was always changing; indeed, it's still a matter of controversy today.

There is a sentiment that began with Yellowstone that plays into Turner's ideas: If the wild West is what made us who we are today, should we let it all vanish? Shouldn't we preserve parts of it that can act as a memory of what the country once was, and to imagine what it would be to re-create that experience? In part, that's what the national parks were set up to do. But how do you re-create this older experience, and bring new people into the parks, and save wild nature at the same time? And what happens once you set up the parks, if you begin changing the land itself?

Q: In our discussion of icons, we left out one contemporary icon, and that's the Marlboro Man. How, how has he hung on so long?

A: Well, in the end, the great icon of the American West ends up being the cowboy. The odd thing about the cowboy as a cultural icon is that he emerges so late. He really didn't become very powerful until the end of the nineteenth century, when the open-range cattle industry that produced the cowboy was dead. So it's an icon that emerged as the real cowboy vanished. But once that icon had emerged, you had a figure who could encapsulate virtually all the figures that have gone before him. He takes in the scout, he takes in the pioneer. He really ended up becoming this strong, individual, white male, who stands alone against the wilderness and all dangers. The cowboy sums up American individualism. He sums up this sense of a man who's got to do what he's got to do and is capable of doing it. Once that icon had developed, it could be imagined or identified with by all kinds of Americans whose actual lives reflect nothing of being a cowboy. But there are moments in everyone's life when you imagine taking your fate in your own hands, depending on nobody but yourself and being out there against the elements—and all of that is in the cowboy. The cowboy still is capable of reflecting those values today. It's no mystery that many people who want to sell a product or push a point of view on the American public have tried to tag it on to the cowboy. He has become an incredibly powerful cultural figure.

The interesting thing is that the historical cowboy often worked for a corporation. He was hardly a lone individual—he worked for a wage. One of the interesting things is that he's the only wage earner I know who's become an iconic figure in the West. And most of the time, he chased cows. I mean, it was not particularly romantic labor.

Nonetheless, all that can be stripped away. It's what you stand for, not what you actually do, that matters.

Q: But using myths makes life bearable, doesn't it?

A: Absolutely. Even if I could get rid of myths, I wouldn't want to. You can't understand history without understanding myths, because people don't mold their lives according to what actually happened. They mold their lives according to what they think happened. And what they think happened is encapsulated in myths.

In a lot of ways, Americans act out the West in modern life. When Europeans will dismiss Ronald Reagan's diplomacy as cowboy diplomacy, when Henry Kissinger allows himself to be described as the sheriff striding into town to clean up the world, what we have is American public figures, political figures, acting according to a mythological script that was written out in the West. To understand them, you have to understand that myth. So I'm in favor of understanding all this, not debunking it. And I don't think the myths are ever going to disappear. They're the stories that we tell ourselves to make sense of our world.

Q: You were a major consultant and a source for Ken Burns's PBS show *The West*. Tell me what you learned about how filmmakers approach history as opposed to the way historians approach history.

A: I learned a lot. I learned to appreciate what it's like to tell stories with films. Films do simplify history in a way that many academic historians find alarming, but I think it's necessary if you're going to be able to tell a powerful story through film. Films also personalize everything. Historians want to deal with large factors that affect many people. But films, by and large, have to be about people. They have to encapsulate things. And they always have to tell a story.

Once I learned how films are put together, I began to appreciate them much more. Now, most academic historians really believe that if we were allowed to make films, we'd do a much better job. But, really, if we were allowed to make films, nobody would watch them. I'm certain of that. What many of my colleagues think is that films should sort of be monographs shown on TV, and you can't end up doing that.

Q: So do you think that *The Civil War* and *The West* series and serious historical productions on television are worth the effort and the money that goes into them, or is it distorted history?

A: This may be misunderstood, but all history is distorted history.

Q: Even yours?

A: Even mine. There's no God's-eye view of the world. When we write history, we have to leave things out, and what you leave out is critical to the kind of history you write. So you're always writing from a certain perspective. You tell the truth, you match the story against the sources, but you always write from a certain perspective.

So film history, like any history, is distorted. But when it's good, it's very, very good. It's different from academic history, it's different from written history. But I always remind my colleagues is that in my twenty minutes in *The West*, I reached more people—more people by a multiple of thousands—than I will in all of my historical writing. I'd say that the way history reaches most people in the late twentieth and early twenty-first centuries is going to be through film and through TV, that is simply the way things are.

Q: So what was it in the beginning that drew you to the West, aside from living out there? What is it about the West that captured you?

A: Well, what captured me first was history in general, and it captured me in an odd way. My mother is an Irish immigrant, my grandparents were Jewish immigrants from Russia. And so I always had a set of stories of their past, which was very different from the past where I was growing up. So as a child, I was always interested in how that change took place, and I was aware that the past was a strange place, a place that I was in no way familiar with.

I became interested in history because my family was new to the country in my own personal background. I became intensely interested in American history and American stories. And in the end, the stories that were the most compelling to me were stories about the West. When I moved West myself, it only became more compelling. Then in my late teens I began to meet Indian people, and I saw them not as these romantic relics of the past but as political actors, people engaged in their community, involved in fishing-rights demonstrations. I worked with Navajo workers at canneries, and I became very interested in Indian peoples as living people in the West. And out of that came my adult career.

Q: You say that you became interested in storytelling

and the great stories of your family and the West, and yet so many academic historians don't tell stories, do they?

A: I know what you mean, but I think academic historians are telling more stories than they did in the past. Sometimes they boil down to very bad stories, not very compelling stories.

It seems to me if you're trapped in storytelling, it's not necessarily such a bad trap. That's just a way that we understand the world, and we should tell the best, most compelling stories we can. I want my stories to be as inclusive as they possibly can be, to speak to the widest possible audience they can, and I want them to be rigorous. And that's a real challenge for academic historians. It's a challenge that, by and large, academic historians have not met, though there are some notable exceptions. And I think that very much should be our goal.

CHAPTER FOUR

David McCullough
on the Industrial Era

Although David McCullough is one of the most distinguished historians working today, he has received no formal training in the discipline and considers himself primarily a writer and a storyteller. He is the recipient of numerous awards, among them a Pulitzer Prize for the universally acclaimed *Truman,* his most recent book (which was ten years in the making), and National Book Awards for *The Path Between the Seas,* an epic chronicle of the creation of the Panama Canal, and *Mornings on Horseback,* a biography of the young Theodore Roosevelt—all of which were bestsellers. He has also published books about the Johnstown flood and the Brooklyn Bridge, and essays on historic figures past and present. Millions of television viewers know David McCullough as the host of *The American Experience* and as the narrator of numerous PBS documentaries, including *The Civil War.* He recently served as the president of the Society of American Historians and is currently at work on a book about the intertwining lives of John and Abigail Adams and Thomas Jefferson.

Q: How would you describe the Industrial Age in America—the period of tremendous growth in the late nineteenth and early twentieth centuries?

A: Somebody asked Theodore Roosevelt, "How have you been able to do all these things, write books, and run for public office, be a soldier, and be a naturalist, and be an outdoorsman, and so forth and so on?" And he said, "I put myself in the way of things happening, and things happen." And he lived in a "things happening" time in the late nineteenth century. That big period between the end of the Civil War and the start of World War I was one of the most active, contrasting, extreme, and audacious periods in our whole history, and it was very American, it seems to me.

Because suddenly all this variety of talent, variety of background, variety of ambitions came together and produced a revolutionary change. The paleontologists, the people who study evolution, talk about a process called "punctuated equilibrium," which says that evolution doesn't happen gradually. Instead, it comes in bursts, in these sudden surges where change in the form of the species is very noticeable. It happens sometimes in a very brief time, as geologic times goes. And that's the way it was after the Civil War and before World War I.

We tend to associate that period, as we should, with mechanical and scientific changes: the advent of the telephone and the typewriter and the automobile and electricity and the electric light, and the coming of the railroads and the invention of dynamite. And there were huge changes in medicine. Clean surgery had its origins in this time. You have the building of the skyscraper— one of the most important events in world history, not just American history.

But we tend to forget how protean, how productive, how creative that time was in the arts. Architecture was

one obvious field, but also this was the time that produced Walt Whitman. This was the time that produced
Thomas Eakins. This was the time that produced
Winslow Homer and Mark Twain. *Huckleberry Finn,*
maybe our greatest novel, came out of this period. So it
was a very creative, interesting time.

Q: Were the developments all so positive?

A: Oh, hardly. There were some terrible goings-on.
There were rotten politics and dreadful destruction of
the forests, of the buffalo, and of the Native American.
There were awful child labor, terrible working conditions, violent paralyzing strikes, awful slums created
with the invention of the tenement—and people talk
about national problems today. Imagine if half of our
cities today were armed camps, and they were being
burned down. The railroad strike of 1877—one of the
worst, the darkest moments in the entire history of the
country—was like that. So all that was going on, but in
the midst of it all, people were getting more of the good
things of life—more abundance, more advantages and
benefits from a civilization than ever before in history.

And, of course, it's the time of the great burgeoning of
the American city as the center of creative energy. There
were huge migrations going on. There were the migrations from Europe, during which eleven thousand people
came into New York in one day in 1911. A million people
came in 1907. It was just a tide of human migration. And
then there was all the migration to the West, which has,
of course, become a big part of our mythology.

But maybe the most important migration of all was
the migration from country to city. People with talent,

people with ambition, people with ideas, people with high hopes were all going to the city, all with the old American sense that "I can do something on my own merit in this kind of country." The city was where the opportunity was.

Q: But there's a sense that that period from the Civil War up to the twentieth century was sort of a dismal period in American history. It's almost forgotten in many histories, which jump from the Civil War right to World War I.

A: You may be right. And I think one of the reasons was that for a very long time there was an attitude on the part of historians that history was only about politics and the military. And politics and the military in that period are really not very interesting. From Abraham Lincoln to Theodore Roosevelt, there was a pretty bland lineup of presidents; very few people can keep them straight. There's almost no one very interesting.

And in the military, of course, there was very little of note except its often disgraceful performance in the West. But if you see history as much more than politics and the military, which is really the only way to see it, then you realize how much was going on, and how our own time has its roots back then.

Q: In what way?

A: Well, of course, we have roots in the eighteenth century, in the founding of the Republic. But we were really shaped when the machine came into its own. The machine is the great metaphor. You probably remember those pictures of the giant steam engine at the 1876 world's fair, which had something like thirteen acres of machinery, eight thousand different machines, sawing wood and printing newspapers and making pins and all kinds of things. The machine was truly the icon of the age. And the effect of Jules Verne was great. Everything was possible now that we had these newfound powers of science and technology. We had powers that had hitherto only been conferred on the gods, and we could do anything.

Eighteen sixty-nine, which I think is one of the most important years in history, was the year of the opening of the Suez Canal and the completion of the transcontinental railroad. And suddenly, as Jules Verne dramatically conveyed in *Around the World in 80 Days,* the world had gotten much smaller. There was no end to what you could do. You could go to the moon, if everything kept going the way it was. And the sense that tomorrow could be, might be, better than today was very powerful at that time, and that's good for a society.

Q: I once heard you say that the men of the 1880s and '90s believed in vision. They believed in possibility. They believed in the perfectibility of society, and they believed in education as the basis of progress. Do you think the men and women of the 1990s still believe that?

A: Yes, I do, but I think we have somehow forgotten that we, too, can be a founding society. We can be a founding era.

If you look at that period one hundred years ago, there were things that were accomplished in that period that transcended that time, and they will be eternals. Homer's paintings, the Brooklyn Bridge, the work of Louis Sullivan and the whole concept of a new kind of building, the poetry of Whitman—that all rises up out of a time when, not only did people have an experimental, creative attitude, but they believed that if something was wrong, they could fix it. They could get rid of child labor. They could clean up the production of canned foods and meats and drugs. They could create labor unions.

One of my favorite quotes of the whole time was a remark attributed to an engineer named John Fritz, who was involved with the creation of the Bessemer steel process. One of the most important events in our history is the advent of cheap steel. It changed everything much more than any politician or any war. It changed the world. Well, Fritz was in Johnstown, Pennsylvania, and they built a machine for the new Bessemer process there. They had been working on it for months. Finally he said, "All right, boys, she's done. Let's start her up, and see why she doesn't work."

That's a very nineteenth-century American attitude. They weren't just thinking about the finished product. They were thinking about the process of creating something by finding out why it didn't work.

And in the nineteenth century in politics, in the Progressive Era, they were saying, "This is not working. So we'll fix it and make it work." It's why the Americans succeeded in building the Panama Canal, and the French didn't. The French were doing everything by the book, and the book didn't work. The Americans went down there, and they were empirical. "We'll do what works. We'll improvise." That attitude is in jazz. It's all through our society. And the engineers on the canal kept improvising until they saw why it wasn't working, and they saw the solution, and it worked.

Q: Do you think this country could have done what it did without this steady wave of immigrants?

A: No. Impossible. America needed all that. It needed it, first of all, as a labor source. It needed cheap labor. But they also had that yeast coming in in the cultural backgrounds. You see it in Willa Cather's novels, where she talks about the Bohemians, and what they're bringing to this society on the Great Plains of Nebraska. We are so indebted to the cultures from which we all come, much more than we realize. And it will take another fifty years or more maybe before we begin to see that.

Q: Do you think we are absorbing immigrants in the twentieth century as successfully as we absorbed them in the nineteenth century?

A: No, we're not. And I think we're being short-sighted if we don't realize to what degree great talent is coming in with people who are not ostensibly talented—people who don't come because they have a Ph.D. in physics and they have more opportunity here. Those people are very important, but the real talent is probably going to come from someplace else. If you keep people under a lid for generations, and then take that lid off, something happens. It's from those groups that the real talent will come. Generally speaking, in our society, more than any that's ever existed, talent comes to the fore. And I don't just mean talent to paint pictures or to play the piano. I mean talent to do all kinds of things.

Q: The talent to build our own nation.

A: That's right. And what's so interesting to me in an accomplishment, like, say, the building of the Brooklyn Bridge or the Panama Canal or the rise of an individual politician, is how many different kinds of talents are involved to make that happen. It isn't just the engineer. It isn't just the designer. Of course, there's the driving adrenaline of wanting to be useful. This was a society where you could be useful. "Hey, we need you. Come over here and help do this." And in America we judge people in the really democratic ethic, we judge people by their work.

That's why baseball is such a wonderful metaphor for the country, because what matters is how you do the job out there on that field. It doesn't matter who you are, where you came from, who you know, how much education or little education you had, as long as you do the job. And that's all through our society, and we're at our best when we're remembering that.

War brings it out, and it's too bad that that has to be so. War does galvanize a sense that everybody can play a part and everybody has value and everybody can be a hero and everybody can be of benefit. What we need to find are great, unifying, constructive goals, ideals that can call on that same kind of creative energy.

Q: Just listening to you talk, and also reading what

you have written, I'm struck by your exuberance. You have so much optimism that I wonder whether that's affected your choice of subjects.

A: I don't think that one can see the light in life without the shadow. And there's great shadow in the story of the past, in all parts of the world. I hope I have been not just aware of all that, but that I have recorded it. I am, however, particularly drawn to those stories, those events, those lives, wherein the human spirit is victorious in the end. They're not necessarily victorious as society judges victory, and they're often the people who don't usually figure in history with a capital *H*. I think people are the most interesting subject of all, and I am thoroughly interested in those people who went before us.

Of course, I draw a great pleasure from history. It's all well and good to say that "we should know history because it makes us better citizens," and it does. And that "there are great lessons in history," and there are. But history is also a source of immense pleasure in the way that music and art and the theater can be sources of great pleasure. We shouldn't deny ourselves that pleasure, and we shouldn't deny our coming generations from that pleasure.

Q: Do you ever wish you'd lived in the last quarter of the nineteenth century?

A: I'd like to go there for a couple of days, certainly.

Q: Just a couple of days?

A: Yes. I think we're living right now in one of the most interesting of all times. If living back then meant that I couldn't live now, I would definitely stay here.

I would hate to have to face the kind of dentistry they had then. And I probably wouldn't have had a chance to see as much of the world as I have been able to do, and there are all kinds of reasons. It would have been very much harder to make a living then. We have so many more opportunities, so much more variety or choice of vocation, which is one of the points I try to make when I visit college campuses. I tell students: "Don't think for a minute that you have a choice of five things you can do; there's five hundred fifty or fifty-five hundred choices."

But, yes, I'd certainly like to go there for a time. I feel that one can be provincial in time, as much as one can be provincial in a geographic way. And why cut ourselves off from that larger experience of all of those who went before us? The books and the biographies and the autobiographies and motion pictures and all the rest are there to take us back into that other time. I can't imagine anybody who wouldn't want to be a time traveler, at least part of their life. There's so much to learn, and there's so much that's advantageous to know from history.

History is mostly, it seems to me, a lesson in proportions. You think times are tough? You think you are beset by adverse luck? Others have had it worse. Others have gone through worse. Others have triumphed over many more difficult obstacles. We think we're superior, because we live in this miraculous twentieth century. I don't think anybody can feel superior standing in front of some of the great works of Botticelli, let's say, in the Uffizi Gallery in Florence, or standing in front of the Golden Gate Bridge, one of the most magnificent creations of human ingenuity and imagination that I know of.

Q: You once said that your style, your technique, was having one subject sort of lead you to another?

A: Yes.

Q: Your first book was on the Johnstown flood. How did you get from the Johnstown flood to the Brooklyn Bridge?

A: The Johnstown flood is a fascinating subject. You asked me if I consider the darker aspects of history. Well, the Johnstown flood is really a lesson, a morality lesson about our pathetic human inclination to think that because people are in positions of responsibility, they are, therefore, behaving responsibly.

The Johnstown Flood is a story of human short-sightedness, selfishness. It's trouble brought on by human frailty and flaws. And after I wrote *The Johnstown Flood,* I was looking for a symbol of affirmation, because it's really a very discouraging story. And I had two publishers come to me: One wanted me to write about the Chicago fire, and the other wanted me to do the San Francisco earthquake. And I said to myself, I'm going to be typecast as "Calamity McCullough."

So I was looking for a subject where human beings in a cooperative concerted effort did something right. It was not easy finding one. Suddenly I thought—the Brooklyn Bridge, this wonderful American triumph, this great achievement, which was only possible because of corruption and the bad people who were mixed up in it. You know, nobody wants to write about saints. I was thrilled every time I could write about Boss Tweed, because he's rotten, and he's charming, and he's effective, and he's human.

But out of all this amalgam of idealism and ambition and greed and political corruption and courage—I think more than anything it's a story of courage—out of that comes this superlative work, great work of art, great work of engineering, great event in the history of the American city. Here's steel being used in a high-rise structure for the first time. The bridge was the beginning of heroic New York—high-rise New York—and there it stands today still. It was built in the horse-and-buggy days, built when all those rivets were hand-thrown. When they went down into the caissons, there was no communication from aboveground to below water, because there was simply no way to do that.

And they didn't know they were going to succeed. Of course, nor did the Founding Fathers who were at Philadelphia in 1776 know they were going to succeed. In fact, there was every reason to believe they weren't going to succeed. That's why it's so important to put yourself in their place, in their time, to perceive reality as they saw it. That makes what they did seem all the more extraordinary. When you think of what these people did and what they were, it can make you feel like you're a pygmy in comparison, because of how much they accomplished in a single life.

Diversion hadn't become an industry yet in American life. Today we have these huge combinations of talent and money all bent on diverting us from life. People couldn't tune out boredom in those days. In those days you either sat there and you were bored, or you did something. And a lot of people did something. I like that.

Another pull for me in many of my subjects is that when I started out, I didn't know a thing about that particular topic. I wasn't an expert on any subject that I ever undertook as a book. Had I been thoroughly knowledgeable in the subject, I think I wouldn't have wanted to write the book, because then the four years, the five years, the ten years that it takes to research it wouldn't have been the adventure that it was when I was exploring it for the first time.

Q: You said that just looking at the Brooklyn Bridge made you feel good.

A: It still does.

Q: It does?

A: Oh, indeed, it does. It is this triumphant structure, rising up out of those cities, rising up out of that distant time, telling us that we can build, we can do things well, and that we have a long life, that we are enduring. Now, because the Brooklyn Bridge has survived, because it was so superbly constructed, because it was so beautifully built, because the engineers who designed it did have a sense of responsibility, doesn't mean that that's representative of that age. Because bridges were falling down all over the place then, to a much greater degree than they do today.

What the Brooklyn Bridge is saying is that if you really care about who you are and what you do, about what your work is, you will want it to stand out through ages as what you did. That civilization is saying to us, "This is the best we can do, and it is very good."

We should be in awe of those people and of that structure. Not in awe of them because they were closer to the angels than we are, but because they could rise up and do something like that. The bridge represents a collective effort drawing on ideas and ideology and aspirations that come from elsewhere, built by immigrants who did the hard labor at the risk of their lives, and designed by a German immigrant, John Roebling, but carried on by his son.

The father, the old man, who was a tyrannical, violent, iron-willed, humorless, and sometimes abusive man, was the great suspension-bridge genius of the nineteenth century. He died in 1869, just as the bridge was about to begin. He was killed as a consequence of an accident, died of lockjaw—a terrible way to die, an awful death. And his son took over. His son was then in his thirties and most of the engineers who worked on that bridge were young men. The average age was about thirty-two. And, in a way, that's a metaphor for our society, our country. The Founders, if you will, created the plan, the ideal concept. But then they went away, and it's been up to us to try and make it work, to build a nation.

But John Roebling left a lot of problems that he hadn't worked out, just as the Founders of our society left a lot of problems that we still haven't worked out in some cases. And, so, to me, the Brooklyn Bridge is a very American story.

Q: Did you have a particular interest in engineering when you began that book?

A: I had no interest in engineering or mathematics. But I did find out that if you're motivated, if you want to know how something was done, if you want to understand physics and mathematics and civil engineering, you can do it. You can do it because you're learning it yourself, which is different from having somebody just tell it to you. And when you learn things that way—by doing it yourself, figuring it out yourself—you learn it in a way that you never forget.

Q: Villanova gave you an honorary doctorate in engineering.

A: It did, and so did RPI, which really floored my father, because he was very mathematical and loved engineering, and he knew that I very nearly didn't get into college because I did so poorly on the physics side of the college board exam.

I'm not an engineer, and I haven't been a bridge buff, and I certainly had no past history and interest in canals, but the Panama Canal book and the Brooklyn Bridge book were exciting adventures for me because I got to know those people. One of the advantages is that unlike politicians and military heroes, they didn't have the sense that, "Oh, I'm going to be a figure in history. So I'm going to write this letter. I'm going to keep this diary so some future historian will admire me for what I'm saying, and how I'm behaving." Those engineers didn't see their role in quite that way. So their letters, their diaries, their stories are often much more genuine, not so self-conscious.

Q: What's the cultural significance of the Panama Canal? I know it saved a lot of shipping time, but what did it mean for America to have built that?

A: Well, the fact that the French had failed, I think,

was a very powerful motivating force because we were going to pick up where Europe had not done the job, and we were going to show them that we could do it.

The lesson to be learned from the Panama Canal is that it succeeded by taking its greatest problem and making the problem an advantage. The problem was the rainfall and the Chagres River. The region had some of the heaviest rainfall anywhere in the world. The Chagres River was a surging monster, a lion in the path, as they said. That river could rise twenty, twenty-five feet in twenty-four hours, and how in the world were they going to get through that? How were they going to divert it or tunnel under it or bridge over it? The French never could figure it out, which was ironic because one of their own engineers told them how to do it before they even began. The key was not to try to dig a Suez-type of canal, a great sea-level trench from ocean to ocean, but to create a lock-and-lake canal, where the ships are lifted up by a series of locks to a man-made lake, and then they sail across that lake, and then they are set back down on the other side by another series of locks. So it becomes a bridge of water. Well, the source of the water is the Chagres. So what makes the thing work is that the Chagres River is a constant, torrential, never-ending supply of water. You work with the problem, work with nature in order to create the best engineering.

It was exactly the way a jujitsu perfectionist uses his opponent's strength to overcome his opponent. And I think we really could apply that attitude toward lots of problems that we have. That the solution to the problem is in the problem, the so-called problem. It's no longer a problem if you see it that way.

It's incredible that we went to Panama, two thou-

sand miles from our source of supplies, brought everything there, and confronted the diseases that were
there. And, of course, disease is a huge and powerful
force in history. One of the most important of all forces
in history is the ravaging effect and consequences of
epidemic disease: yellow fever and malaria, in particular. We don't have our capital in Philadelphia because
they had a great yellow fever epidemic. We conquered—
if that's the word—both yellow fever and the malaria in
Panama.

We did build a lock-and-lake canal. We didn't try to
cut through the isthmus at sea level. We would have
failed had we tried to do that. We built the canal for less
than it was estimated to cost, and we did it with a serious loss of life—but not the loss of life that the French
experienced. The French lost twenty thousand people,
trying to build the Panama Canal. We lost about five
thousand.

Q: Really?

A: Twenty-five thousand human beings died trying
to build that canal. But it was a triumph for us. When
the French went to Panama, they went in reaction to
the Franco-Prussian War, which was really a world war.
It was the first war between Germany and France, and
the French were just defeated instantly. It was a deba-
cle. It was a terrible humiliation. And they were going
to try and redeem French honor by going out to
Panama, this dangerous place, and winning a great victory of peace. This was what those young engineers believed when they went out there, knowing they would
probably die.

And yet they believed in it so fervently that they were willing to go, and most of them did die. The heroism of the French and the lessons that they taught us by their failure—why it didn't work—made it possible for us to succeed. They showed us if we didn't solve the disease problem, and if we had the intelligence not to try and dig a sea-level canal, we might prevail. And we would have to finance it by the government, because there wasn't private financing big enough to float it. The failure of the French Canal Company was the biggest financial collapse of the nineteenth century. It rocked the whole government of France. It gave rise to the anti-Semitism in France that eventually resulted in the Dreyfus case.

Q: I suppose, then, the canal got you moved toward Teddy Roosevelt?

A: Yes. There is a line of progression. A large part of the story of the Johnstown flood is the Pennsylvania Railroad, and the Pennsylvania Railroad was surveyed through Johnstown by John Roebling, who built the bridge. And when I was writing about the Brooklyn Bridge, one of the events of the time in New York was that Ferdinand de Lesseps came to New York to pump up an interest in his stock company to build the Panama Canal.

When I did the Panama Canal book, I ran into Theodore Roosevelt, and I got very interested in what he didn't say about his life in his own autobiography. You know, what people leave out is often very important. And while doing Roosevelt didn't lead me directly to Truman, it did lead me to this office we call the presidency. I became fascinated by its possibilities and how some people who don't seem to promise a great deal can suddenly do exceptional things.

Q: The Roosevelt family was part of the Knicker-bocker aristocracy, which was as close to a true aristoc-racy as we ever had in America.

A: Yes. Well, there were important aristocracies in a few American cities at that time. The great difference with the Roosevelts is that they were in New York, and they had the money and the power of New York. In fact, the advent of New York City is one of the most impor-tant stories in our whole history. And if you had an aris-tocracy in New York, that was in a different league.

The Roosevelts were, to a large degree, rather pro-saic, stay-at-home, moneymaking, conservative people of a somewhat narrow perspective. Theodore Roosevelt is, in truth, in my view, much more like his mother, who was a Bulloch from Georgia. They were romantic, ec-centric daredevils, adventurous, brave, and lovable, in their way. I'm not sure how lovable some of those old Roosevelt Dutchmen were.

Q: Did they really speak Dutch at the dinner table?

A: In the grandfather's house, yes.

Q: And why didn't any of the Roosevelt men fight in the Civil War?

A: Well, as you know, in those days, you could purchase a substitute, hire somebody to go in your place, and that was done by a lot of people. There was no social stigma attached to it.

Q: They were draft dodgers, weren't they?

A: In fact, they were draft dodgers, but the draft dodging was limited to people who were wealthy enough to afford it. Grover Cleveland did the same thing. It's important that Theodore Roosevelt senior, the father of the president, hired a substitute. He gave all kinds of reasons for that, which I'm sure were sincere. He was married to a southern woman. The idea that he might be going off to fight her brothers would have just killed her. He was also responsible for a large family, and he was involved in the creation of what we would now call the Red Cross for the troops.

But what's important about his action is that to his son, Theodore, this was the one flaw, the one disappointing passage in the life of his father, who was his hero all of his life. And I don't like to use psychological jargon, but, to a degree, one could say that Theodore Roosevelt was compensating, trying to compensate for that aspect of his father's life by wanting to get in every war that ever was, and to show what a hero and courageous fellow he could be.

Q: As the biographer of Teddy Roosevelt, what do you think of President Clinton's attempt to remake himself in the image of Teddy Roosevelt.

A: I didn't know that he was trying to do that.

Q: That's the line, that he was looking for a presidency in which, as you mentioned, there was no war. A presidency in which the man distinguished himself by his character, rather than the events around him.

A: I think the presidents who do best are the presidents that are just themselves, that don't try to be like somebody else, because that's not a very effective way to accomplish anything or to lead. Nobody can be like Theodore Roosevelt. He and Clinton are both Olympic talkers, though; I will say that.

Theodore Roosevelt was an eccentric. If he were around today, people would really wonder about him. I think he was a genius. He could read two books in a night, and quote from them five years later. He could recite all of the *Song of Roland* in its original archaic French. He knew all about the big vertebrates of North America, probably as much as any zoologist at the Smithsonian, maybe more. He wrote—I don't know—some twenty-two books. He embraced life with such zest, and he exuded such confidence and optimism that people would at times incline to believe that that was the whole man.

It was not at all. He had a very deep melancholy and a withdrawing quality where he would go into a dark room and close the door and sit and read the poetry of Edward Arlington Robinson, which is very down, blue, dark. He closed off whole sides of his personal life, and wouldn't talk about it, because that was his way of coping with it.

He's complicated and interesting. The John Singer Sargent portrait, I think, captures that. There's a wistful sort of sad quality in that portrait that's missing in the usual photograph of the grinning, toothy, fist-waving Theodore Roosevelt. Sargent saw something that was much closer to the real man.

Q: How do you think future biographers will look at us?

A: Future biographers and historians are going to have an impossible time writing about us. We don't write letters. We don't keep diaries. They are going to think we talked like business memoranda, which is a great shame.

They are going to have lots of photographs, and if they save the outtakes from television interviews, they may have some material there. But one of the joys of the nineteenth century is that they wrote so well, and they wrote so often. And newspapers in that era still hadn't the technology to reproduce photography, so that the descriptive account of events—a great fire or a flood or a funeral—were all very pictorial in the writing, and there were many more newspapers. So they were very competitive, and you have lots to choose from.

To write about the nineteenth century is really a dream, because there's just a surplus of riches of all kinds—photographs, diaries, letters, privately published memoirs, and those newspapers and the magazines. Because it was such a great era of new magazines starting up and wonderful writing and wonderful writers. It was a very creative time.

Q: Reading *Mornings on Horseback*, your biography

of young Teddy Roosevelt, I was filled with awe at the letters that his mother wrote, and the diary that he kept, never missing a day—with the acute observations of a ten-year-old boy.

A: Yes. Of course, the Puritans all kept diaries as a way of measuring if they were improving, to sort of examine themselves. So the diary tradition is very deep in American life, and it starts to fade out, I suppose, with the advent of the telephone.

But Theodore Roosevelt's command of the language is exceptional. He had the advantage of a Harvard education and of growing up in a house with books and cultivated people. What, to me, is maybe more striking is the quality of the prose of what one would assume to be everyday people.

For example, when I was working on my book about the Panama Canal, I read the reports of the young naval officers who went to the Isthmus of Panama and Mexico and elsewhere, looking for the best route to build the canal. Those reports are wonderfully written, and they didn't have any public relations department at the navy to brush this prose up.

Samuel Eliot Morison, once talking about the decline of the quality of the oratory on the floor of the Congress and Senate in Washington, said that he thought it could be dated from the time that Latin was no longer required in the schools. His generation was raised on Latin and on the models of Bunyan, *Pilgrim's Progress,* Shakespeare, and some very good poets, and it rubbed off. They couldn't spell to save their lives (which is, I think, quite endearing, because I'm sympathetic to that problem). But Jefferson, Adams, they couldn't spell at all. In fact, Andrew Jackson said he would never trust a man that could have so little imagination as to be able only to spell a word in one way.

Q: As a historian, does it ever worry you that comparing the way things actually happened with the way people *said* they happened will lead you to mistakes?

A: Yes, indeed. And there are many times when you're like the umpire at home plate with a very close call, and you have to call it. Sometimes you're wrong. Sometimes you make a mistake. It's less of a problem than you think, though, because there are so many accounts of the same incident, and so many documents on paper.

A big part of writing a book, a biography or history, is in what's called in too fancy a way, the analysis. You collect all of the material. That's the research, and that's wonderful fun. That's joy. That's like working on a detective case. The hard stuff is the writing. And there's that point where you have to take all this material you've gathered and put it out on the table—and look at it and think about it. That's why the books take so long. You have to think so much about it. And writing is thinking. That's what makes it so hard. And to write well is really to think clearly.

I used to think that the way to do this is that you gather all the research and then you simply write the book. But I've found that is not the best way to do it, at least for me. Because it's only when you start writing that you find out what you don't know. You find out what you need to know. And you find yourself coming to conclusions or having insights that you don't have unless you write. Because the process of the writing forces you to think about it, and sometimes gives rise to inspiration.

Q: What kind of standards do you have as a historian?

A: I like to think my standards are every bit as high as those of anyone, concerning the depth of the research, the breadth of the research, the capacity to analyze what I bring to the table from the research.

The great difference, I expect, is that I'm writing for you. I'm writing for everybody. I'm not writing just for other historians. I couldn't survive if my books weren't read. Now I've never tried to take subjects that would be popular or to write in a popular way. There's no need to gussy it all up, and somehow sugar the pill or whatever. You don't have to do that.

I remember, in some instances, when I told people what I was going to be working on, they would say, "Well, who would want to read about that?" If the story pulls me, if I'm excited about it, then my hope is that I can find some readers who will also feel the same way. I'm a narrative historian.

Q: Define narrative history for me.

A: It unfolds as the events unfolded at the time, and you're inside the narrative, the story. You are not seeing it from the grand mountaintop, or the grand advantage of the present, looking out over the past and pontificating about it. You are in the event. You are inside that time. I want a reader to have the feeling of having lived in a distant, different, vanished time. And I want a reader to sense that those were real human beings, and that they didn't know how it was going to come out, any more than we do in our time.

Q: But you know how it came out.

A: I do know how it came out. If I'm writing about the building of the Brooklyn Bridge, for example, I know that the bridge gets built. But I want the reader at some point early in that book to say, "I wonder if they're going to be able to do it" or "How are they going to do it?" And that's going to be revealed by their story, and it will be revealed as it happens to the people in the story.

I don't want the reader to think of their time as past. There isn't really, if you think about it, there isn't any such thing as the past. The people in the story didn't live in the past. They didn't walk around and say, "Oh, isn't this fascinating, living in this great old time?" They lived in the present, *their* present. Now, their present was different from our present, and more different than we know.

The hardest thing to convey in writing history or teaching history is that nothing ever had to happen the way it happened. It could have gone off in any number of different directions at any point, for any number of different reasons. But the tendency in teaching history or writing history is to say, this followed this, this followed that, and that's the way it was. As if it was all on a track and was preordained. And you better memorize it, because there's going to be a test on it on Wednesday.

But that isn't the way it happened. Think of the history you've seen. You have witnessed things suddenly take a swerve in a direction that nobody had ever expected, just as your own individual life can do that. That's exactly the way it was for them.

Q: Can you give an example?

A: In the nineteenth century, for example, when the world was all sort of giddy over the ideal and the promise of progress, they didn't know that World War I was just over the horizon. They didn't know what the machine gun and poison gas and tanks and all that were going to do. They didn't know that.

But for us to say, "Wasn't that naïve of them to believe in progress?" It wasn't naïve. They were judging from experience. Things were getting better all around them, and there wasn't any reason not to expect that they would continue to get better.

Q: Don't you have to resist the temptation to condemn those people for being naïve?

A: Absolutely. You have to fight what you might call the hubris of the present. The idea that, "Oh, those innocent, ill-informed people. Why didn't they behave more intelligently and fairly and so forth?"

I think if a historian or a biographer could build up a quality in the way one would build up a muscle, it should be the capacity for empathy. Put yourself in their place, in their shoes, in their time. You see it all the time, "Oh, that was a simpler time." There *was* no simpler time. It may seem simpler to us, but it certainly didn't seem simple to them. Some say we live with greater horrors than they did—but is it worse to die with a spear through your chest, or to have gone down in an airplane? I don't know.

We will probably never be able to comprehend, for example, how honest, kind, Bible-reading, decent Americans could actually *own* people. How could they have had slavery? What was on their minds? What was wrong with them? We see that, and we feel that intensely. But you can be sure that someday they're going to look back at us and say "What in the world were they thinking about? What kind of blinders were they wearing?" It's anyone's guess what that will be. I suspect it will be what we're doing to the environment. They'll say "Look what they did. Had they no sense of the time, no sense of responsibility? Look what they did."

Q: Is that why Thomas Jefferson has become "politically incorrect"?

A: Well, some historians seem to have just discovered that Jefferson had slaves. I think that's been known. What is bothersome about Jefferson's position in our life is that he was such a very lofty idealist, and therefore the reality that he was living on the labor of people in bondage, that that provided him with his wealth, his free time to think lofty thoughts, seems a huge contradiction and hypocritical. And it is.

I think Jefferson was in many ways a tragic man, because he was the captive. He kept people in captivity, and he was captive to that way of life that captivity creates. Just as he was, in a way, a captive of the southern tradition of hospitality, generosity. He was giving great parties, everybody was welcome to his house. He served the finest wine. And the man was bankrupt. But he kept on doing this, as if he was incapable of not doing it, because that was the way of life. Just as holding people in slavery was the way of life, and he didn't know how to get out of it.

Q: Was it that the economic necessity of having slaves overcame his moral objections?

A: I think he was fearful that if he let his slaves leave, if he gave them freedom, that they would run into more trouble than as it was. And he certainly would have run into increased economic trouble, because they were his greatest single financial asset.

Q: But he was certainly a contradiction.

A: Everybody is a contradiction within themselves. All of us are inconsistent, contradictory, and at times hypocritical. But when you get these larger-than-life characters, then it sometimes becomes more vivid.

I personally think that Jefferson is perhaps best understood if we see him as an artist. He was, after all, one of the greatest American architects ever. He was very inventive, very imaginative, very creative. Now, when you think of great composers, or great painters or playwrights, they all, in their real life, were hypocritical, contradictory, inconsistent. But Jefferson's idealism flies in the face of that. And one tends to say "Hey, wait a minute."

When one turns to a man like John Adams—who didn't have Jefferson's charm or elegance of bearing, who wasn't handsome, who wasn't tall, who wasn't wealthy, who took his own stand on matters of principles and ideology—and see that he lives up to his preachments, then that's terribly exhilarating to see that.

I think there's too much of a tendency not to give credit where credit is due. We have swung away from the great-man theory of history, which is right. But in going that far, sometimes we tend to forget that there were indeed great men and women who did very great things. That doesn't mean greatness is synonymous with perfection. Often our predecessors were quite imperfect, flawed, their feet were mostly clay—but they rose to greatness and did things for which we are the beneficiaries.

Q: Do you think most of our presidents rose to greatness?

A: There's a theory that we only have great presidents when there's a time of crisis: George Washington, Abraham Lincoln, Franklin Roosevelt, great men, great times, faced with great national crises. But there was no crisis in the time of Theodore Roosevelt. He was a force unto himself. And he changed that office, he changed our attitude as we entered this new twentieth century— or really as we were leaving the nineteenth century, because he was really a nineteenth-century president.

I take the view that the twentieth century began with World War I—Barbara Tuchman called it "a burnt path across history." It's a wonderful image, and that's where it was. Everyone was different after World War I, and the world before World War I is vastly different from the one we know in the twentieth century.

Theodore Roosevelt belongs to that time back before the First World War. And when his son was killed in that war, when he saw that that war was producing a different kind of slaughter, when he realized that heroism as he knew it, in the romantic attitude of going toward your crowded hour, that had been wiped out by the machine gun and poison gas and all the rest, that broke his heart. And he died very soon afterward, an old man at sixty years old.

But when he was in his prime, when he was in the office, he changed the White House. He was like nobody who had ever been there before, and nobody that's ever been there since. And I think he was a genius.

Q: Do you like Harry Truman because he was himself? Is that the quality you admire in him.

A: I liked Harry Truman primarily because he's a great story, a great American story. One of the most interesting men I interviewed about Truman was Alonso Fields, who was the head usher at the White House through many administrations, and he described Harry Truman as "a believable man." And that appealed to me a lot. I liked his backbone, his courage. But I think it's the courage of his convictions that's so appealing. I wanted to focus on a very different kind of American after writing about Theodore Roosevelt. And I don't know why, but I came up with the idea of Harry Truman.

So I went to the Truman Library, and I saw that this fellow had poured himself out on paper; in letters and diaries—heartfelt letters, revealing, genuine, wonderful letters. So much so that even if he hadn't become president, one would be tempted to write a book about this guy out in Missouri who is writing all these letters and trying to win the favor of the girl in town that lived in the big house, who wouldn't pay him much attention. It's just a great story.

He was so candid and so without pretense and without hypocrisy. And then, of course, he goes off to war, and he shouldn't go off to war, because he's too old, and he's a farmer, and his eyes aren't good enough, but he's going to go anyway. I like that.

But, you know, I have to stress that I just don't want to write about people that I think are wonderful. They may have done some wonderful things, but I don't want to write about saints. Heaven help me, I'd much rather write about a good scamp than a saint.

Q: Do you think Harry Truman did more to affect history than, say, Franklin D. Roosevelt?

A: Well, I think Franklin Roosevelt was *the* great president of the twentieth century. I don't think there's any question about that. But I personally like the Truman story. He didn't have the advantages that Roosevelt had, and so there's the adversity that he had to face, the difficulty, the conflict in his life, and could this man rise to the occasion? And he hadn't been the subject of a full biography before, which was very important.

I felt I could break some new ground, and that's very important to a writer always, which was true with the Brooklyn Bridge and the Panama Canal and the Johnstown flood and the early life of Theodore Roosevelt. I was doing something different, and I don't like to repeat myself. I don't want to keep doing the same kind of book. Right now I'm venturing into the eighteenth century, where I've never set foot before. It's all new country to me.

Q: Are there other characters whose lives interest you that you have already decided to write about?

A: Oh, yes. I'm going to have to live about two hundred years, I think, to do it all. But, yes, indeed, there are lots of people I'd love to write about. I keep a running list of ideas for the future. And some of them just sort of drop by the wayside, and then sometimes something will just happen, an impulse, a moment like that Truman idea, and then something just clicks—and that's the book I have to write.

Q: So what are the stories you want to tell now?

A: I'm very interested in the impact of France on America.

Q: Really?

A: I think it's a great story. More American history took place in France than anyplace else in the world except our own country. And the influence of France on our country was immense. When you're working on the Revolutionary War, as I'm doing now, you realize what they did for us. We wouldn't have a country if it wasn't for France. It wasn't just that they sent the fleet and Rochambeau, they bankrolled us. They were supplying money and equipment and all kinds of things when we were in desperate need of it.

I want to cover subjects that should never have come out the way they did. The Revolutionary War is one of them, and the Revolutionary War is the most important war in our history.

Q: You think it is?

A: Oh, yes, indeed. I certainly do. I didn't think that before, but I do now. It changed the world. Thomas Paine was right. We were going to change the world, what happened here was going to change the world. It doesn't have the scale and the grand opera quality of the Civil War. It doesn't have the slaughter of the Civil War, but, proportionately, it was slaughter. I mean we were a very small country. People don't realize how few people there were.

Q: I thought you said that World War I had the most impact.

A: On this century. Yes. And we don't take World War I seriously enough. Because the Second World War was so tumultuous, so god-awful, so massive in its destructiveness that we forget about what happened in World War I. Those hideous battles, and the pell-mell slaughter. It just makes one sick, and no one who had been through that was the same afterward. Nor was the world the same after it.

Q: What is it in our national character that causes Americans to have such a loose grip on their past?

A: We have always been very interested in the future. We greet each other on the street, and I say "What's new?" to you—not, "How are you?" Nobody tells you, "Hey, you know what? I just turned over an old leaf." It's the future. We have always been very future-oriented. We recently had a president win an election about building a bridge to the future—think about tomorrow, think about what's down the road and all that, which is a very American trait, and understandably so. Because the future was going to be better, and we were building for the future.

But what is happening now, I'm sorry to say, is that we are raising a generation of young people who are historically illiterate to a large degree. We've done a very poor job of teaching history and conveying the nature of who we are and how we got to be where we are. And that's bad. We're cutting them off from the pleasure of all that.

Everything we have—our institutions, our material advantages, our laws, our freedom, not to say our poetry, and our music, and our architecture—all comes to us from people who went before us. And to not know anything about them, to be indifferent to them, which is even worse than being ignorant, to be indifferent is really like mass ingratitude.

It's as if something is eating away at the national memory. And, believe me, it's real. What students at good universities and good colleges today don't know about basic American history is appalling.

Q: How did it get that way? I mean, history is required in high school. It's required in grade school.

A: It's not the fault of the students. We got into this situation because in very many cases—in fact, in most cases nationwide—people who are teaching history, particularly in the grade schools, have never had any history. Or if they had history, they didn't like it or weren't good at it. Very often in high school, history is assigned to the coach. He has to teach something, so let him teach history. Now, I happen to have gone to a high school where the coach taught history, and he was a terrific history teacher. I'm not denigrating all coaches.

Q: I was a coach who taught history.

A: You were a coach who taught history?

Q: Right.

A: There's no trick to teaching history. You know that. It's the most appealing subject in the world if it's taught right. But if it's made a matter of dates and memorization of obscure provisos and ancient treaties, if it's made boring, if it's made dull, how can you blame anyone for turning away from it?

Some of the finest writing we have in the English language is in history and biography. That's what students should be reading. And they should have teachers who are excited about the material, who convey their interest, their enthusiasm, their sense of the importance of history. We've got to start early. We've got to start in grade school. We've got to revise, revitalize, improve the teaching of history in the grade school. Because if you get the indoctrination then, if you get the bug then, you're going to have it all your life.

I don't understand anyone who is not interested in history. It's like somebody being color-blind or something. I can't imagine what that's like. And I feel it's such a tragedy when people don't know the past. If you tell someone what happened or what somebody was really like and how they got to be where they were, they say "Well, I never knew that." And it's amazing how many people say to me, "How do you get all the material that's in your books?"—as if nobody has ever told them about going to a library. It's all there.

Q: If you were to teach a course of American history, what half-dozen events or documents could you not leave out?

A: Well, I did teach a course at Cornell University on American history, and I began with the Battle of Gettysburg and I ended with Lyndon B. Johnson, because he was president when my students were born. And I taught each course—each course was a lecture—each lecture, I should say, was not on a subject but on a person or a group of persons. But, of course, by knowing those people, you got to know that subject.

So my first lecture was not about the Battle of Gettysburg. It was about Lee and Longstreet and what happened in three days, and what they did and didn't do because of the kinds of men they were. I did a lecture on Willa Cather, I did a lecture on Roebling, on Washington Roebling and the building of the Brooklyn Bridge. Everything was about a person.

And I gave them a project for their assignment, their term paper, that really was the essence of the course and the essence of what I believe ought to be the way we learn history. Each student—there were 180-some students—was given a photograph. And no two photographs were the same. And the assignment was to write a term paper that derived from that photograph. There was no right or wrong answer. And nobody else in the class was doing the same job, so you weren't competing with other people. You were only competing with yourself.

One student received a Winslow Homer drawing of a Union officer in the Civil War. Another student was given a photograph of an American oil tanker being sunk by a German submarine off the coast of Florida. Another fellow got a photograph of Sergeant York. He may not have even known in what century World War I happened, but he wrote a wonderful paper on Sergeant York. And by learning about Sergeant York, he learned about the whole war.

I was there to help. I said, "You all ought to have back in your rooms one of the greatest research devices ever invented—but you probably never thought of it that way, and you probably haven't been encouraged to think of it that way. It's called the telephone. If you want to find something out, pick up the phone and call somebody who knows the answer." And I encouraged them to go and do interviews. I encouraged them not to just think of conventional research in books and articles and so forth, the kind they're accustomed to doing.

We have wonderful students today, maybe the best ever. But many of them have gotten to where they are because they're very skilled at reading a teacher's mind. And I wasn't going to tell them what I wanted. Some students, I think, discovered that history is great fun. And they changed their major. And in a couple of cases, they found their vocation.

Q: And how did you find your vocation?

A: I found my vocation because I was messing around

up at the Library of Congress one day and I ran across some photographs taken in Johnstown after the flood. And I wanted to know about those photographs, so I took a book out of the library. And one thing led to another, and pretty soon I had gotten very interested in the Johnstown flood, having had no prior interest before that.

People would say, "You must have known a lot about the Johnstown flood before you started off on that project." I said, "No, I didn't." All I knew was that when we were growing up in western Pennsylvania, in Pittsburgh, we used to make a lake of gravy in the mashed potatoes and then we'd take our fork and break it and the gravy would flood down among the peas. And as that happened, we'd say, "The Johnstown flood," not knowing why we did that, not knowing that a dam broke and so forth.

And that's the kick. It's the discovery. It's the adventure that comes with discovery and getting on a project and finding things out yourself. It's suddenly seeing things come into focus and realizing, "Oh, my goodness, look at this. Yes, I see. I understand now." And if it happens that way, you never forget it.

I wrote the Brooklyn Bridge book more than twenty-five years ago, and I'm sure I could go and take a test on it right now and do quite well, because I worked it out myself and, as a consequence, I will never ever forget it. We all know how to cram for an exam. You go in, you spew it out into the blue book, and two weeks later it's gone. Doesn't do any good to teach that way.

Q: Your experience at Cornell must have been really affirming then, wasn't it?

A: Very much so. And it reminded me, and I think reminded the students, that you can do much more than you think you can. I mean, these people were doing good, original, creative research and finding out not only that it was interesting and they wanted to know more about it but that they could do it. And it isn't some mystifying occupation reserved for some great priesthood.

I want everybody to come into the experience of history. E. M. Forster wrote a wonderful book called *Aspects of the Novel,* in which he talks about the difference between a sequence of events and a story. And he says, "If I tell you the king died and then the queen died, that's a sequence of events. If I tell you the king died and the queen died of grief, that's a story." And it's that side of history, the grief, the human experience, that's so essential to get into the writing of history and biography.

I don't think you really know anything until you feel it. It's all well and good to be able to rattle off dates, or the presidents' names, or some Supreme Court decision and its importance and consequence. That's fine. But you ought to also feel it. What did those people go through? What didn't they know? At what cost—knowingly at what cost—were they attempting what they did? And we have to remember that all the people who don't figure in conventional history have a story to tell. They lived lives that were just as real, just as vivid as our own, and in some cases maybe more so.

CHAPTER FIVE

Stephen Ambrose
on World War II
and Postwar America

"I firmly believe that history is chance, just like evolution," Stephen Ambrose once said. "It's not survival of the fittest, it's survival of the luckiest." The stroke of luck that drew him to study World War II was little short of dazzling: Having read Ambrose's first book, Dwight Eisenhower asked the twenty-eight-year-old University of Wisconsin historian to write his biography. Ambrose went on to *Band of Brothers,* about the 101st Airborne, and *D-day June 6, 1944,* and to undertake the revision and updating of the *American Heritage New History of World War II.* His recent *Citizen Soldiers: The U.S. Army from the Normandy Beaches to the Bulge to the Surrender of Germany, June 7, 1944–May 7, 1945* spent time on best-seller lists across the country; his previous book, *Undaunted Courage: Meriwether Lewis, Thomas Jefferson, and the Opening of the American West,* dominated them for months.

Recently retired from his professorship at the University of New Orleans and from the directorship of the Eisenhower Center for American Studies (which he was instrumental in helping found), Ambrose consulted on Steven Spielberg's film *Saving Private Ryan* and saw *Citizen Soldiers* return to the best-seller lists a week after the film opened.

Q: Do you have a clue as to why your book *Undaunted Courage* and, say, Jim McPherson's book *Battle Cry of Freedom* sold so well?

A: Sure. It's a subject I've had to think about. When we were getting ready to publish *Undaunted Courage* in February of 1996, I asked Simon & Schuster, "How many copies?" And they said, "Forty thousand." And I thought, "Well, that sounds about right. That's about what my books sell." I'm a midlist author. But now it's sold over a million. Well, what on earth happened? How could all of us have been so wrong?

I've thought about it, and I realized that if I'd have done that book when I wanted to, in 1976, it would have fallen flat. It would have been a good midlist book. It would have gotten good reviews, it would have been a good book. But it wouldn't have sold twenty thousand. Why the difference twenty years later? Well, in 1976 we had just skedaddled out of Saigon. Nixon had just resigned. The American people were just up to here with cynicism. The last thing they wanted to hear about was heroes.

I began to learn this on the fiftieth anniversary of D-day. With all the hoopla that attended it, the television coverage, it became clear that the American people, twenty years after the fall of Saigon and Nixon's resignation, are yearning for a hero. They're yearning for a sense of national unity. And that's what books like McPherson's *Battle Cry* or my *Undaunted Courage* satisfy. They give readers genuine, authentic heroes, and they bring the country together. They bind us.

Q: Do I quote your wife accurately when she accuses you of—what is it?—"triumphalism"?

A: Yes. My wife and my kids.

Q: What do they mean?

A: They mean I'm celebrating the American past in a negative sense, looking at the good and ignoring the bad. Now, I don't think I'm guilty of that. I mean, I write about Dick Nixon; I write about World War II; I've got American soldiers shooting unarmed German POWs who've got their hands up. These things happened and I report on them.

But, regardless, this is the best country that ever was. This is the freest and, right now, the most prosperous that has ever been conceived anywhere. And, by God, somebody had to be doing something right to bring us to this point. I want to celebrate the people who brought us to this point.

Q: But your books do have a certain sort of six-shooter style to them. Have you abandoned the traditional position of objectivity that historians have had to occupy?

A: I don't really think so. I want to be able to walk in everybody's moccasins. One of the books that I'm proudest of is one called *Crazy Horse and Custer,* and the reason I'm proudest of that is that I've had mail from the Custer fans over the years—and they're real fanatics—saying, "This is good stuff." And I've gotten letters from Sioux Indians and other Indians, saying, "This is the best book I ever read on Crazy Horse." I want to look at it from everybody's point of view. In *Cit-*

izen Soldiers, I wanted the German soldier's point of view as well as the American soldier's point of view. I want to know what it was like.

The thing that drives me as a historian is curiosity. How did they do that? Why did they do that? And sometimes people do terrible things. Well, this is a part of the human condition. War is awful, and I've done most of my writing about war. It's just awful. There's nothing good to be said about it, except that it can't be avoided sometimes.

Q: But you are, as a historian, really taken by war.

A: Yes, for a number of a reasons. First of all, it is the most extreme experience a human being can have—and I've never had it. But I'm fascinated by it. How do men react to being in a foxhole for twenty-four hours, eighteen of them dark? Eighteen of those hours they're in below-zero temperatures, not even able to light a cigarette, but they have to stay alert. And then there are German soldiers coming at them out of the mist at dawn, and so on. How the hell do men do that? That's always fascinated me.

So, I talk to the veterans and I find out how each individual one of them did it, and then I try to make some generalizations about it.

But I'm curious, too, about how men can do awful things. And awful things are done, especially in war, when people shoot unarmed prisoners, when people carry out acts of wanton destruction, when people just go berserk. And this is also a part of what happens in war. I've hated war all my life. I've always been a pacifist.

Q: A pacifist?

A: Oh, yeah. But I also have recognized that war is what determines everything that follows. I mean, it mattered if Joshua Chamberlain held at Little Round Top or not. If he'd have crumbled, and if the Confederates had gotten down into Washington, we'd be in an entirely different world. So, war is decisive in a way that nothing else is. It determines who's going to determine the future.

Q: If you had been, say, with the Twenty-ninth Division on D-day and had gone ashore at Pointe du Hoc or wherever, and survived, would you be writing the same kind of history that you now write?

A: I don't know, I didn't have the experience. But war has driven me. I think it's very deep in our genes. It drove me when I was younger. I think the question most men have is "Am I a coward?" And the only way you can ever find out is to be in combat.

I mean, look at all this stuff that goes on today. We don't have wars anymore, so people are out doing really crazy things. They're skiing, and then they're mountain climbing, and they're ballooning, and all the rest of it. You don't find out if you're a coward or not when you do that. What you find out is if you're a fool or not. But in war you find out if you're a coward. And I never went to war. I was seventeen when the Korean War ended. I never had an opportunity. I probably would have gone as a medic, but it didn't fall to me, or men born at the time I was, to have my country call.

Q: I gather you started as a Civil War historian, did you not?

A: Oh, yes. The man who made me into a historian, Professor William Best Hasseltine, was a Civil War scholar at the University of Wisconsin, where I was an undergraduate.

Q: Your first book was on Henry Halleck, who was Lincoln's chief of staff. How did you get from Henry Halleck in the Civil War to Eisenhower in the Second World War? What happened?

A: Eisenhower read that Halleck book. That was my dissertation. It was published by Louisiana State University Press in an edition of 2,000 copies, and I think they sold 980 of those copies. And maybe half of those 980 were actually read. But one of them was read by Dwight Eisenhower. He read it in 1963, when it came out.

Q: He was the ex-president then?

A: Yes, that's right, living in Gettysburg and out in Palm Springs. He read the book, and he called me. He said, "Would you be interested in being an editor of my papers and my biographer?"

Q: He just called you on the phone and asked you?

A: Yeah. And I said, "Yes, sir!" And flew up to Gettysburg. I was so excited, I didn't need an airplane. I was twenty-eight years old.

So I sat down with him and we talked about it, and what would be involved—all the practical matters. And at the end of a few hours, as we were getting ready to break up, I said, "Sir, why me?" He said, "I read your book on Halleck."

Well, it turned out that he had been thinking about writing on Halleck himself, because he was afraid that George Marshall would be forgotten as Henry Halleck had been forgotten. And he thought if he wrote something on Halleck, it would encourage people to do research and writing on George Marshall, whom he revered, of course.

And when he heard that I had just done a book on Halleck, he said, "Get it to me." And it changed my life. It took me from the Civil War into World War II.

Q: You didn't have any second thoughts about switching from the Civil War period to Eisenhower?

A: None at all. Eisenhower took me into the microfilm room at his office at Gettysburg and said, "Here's some of the material." Some of it was the letters from Eisenhower to Marshall in the spring of 1942, when he talks about the problems he was facing in England. Well, I hadn't read one or two of those letters when I said, "Where do I sign?"

Q: Why did they catch you so strongly?

A: In one of the letters to Marshall, the big dispute was "Are we going to invade in '42 or is it going to be '43, and, if it's '43, what are we going to do in '42?" and so on. Now, I had gone to the University of Wisconsin, and you get an awful lot of influence from the Marxists there. And their view of that part of World War II was Stalin's view. That is, that the Anglo-Americans were sitting on their duffs, doing nothing, while other armies were willing to fight to the last German and the last Russian. And I more or less believed that.

And here I was reading Eisenhower to Marshall in a private letter. In June of 1942, he said, "If we let the Soviet Army go under, it'll be the worst mistake in the whole of human history. We've got to do something to help them." Well, that was a kind of material that nobody had seen before, for goodness' sakes.

Q: One thing has always mystified me about Eisenhower: How could this man, who had been a lieutenant colonel for twenty years, sort of floating in the backwater of the military, how could he suddenly be running the Allied Expeditionary Force in Europe?

A: Well, it wasn't quite that sudden. But you're right; he had been a major for fourteen years. There's a wonderful story from that period. Ike's younger brother, Milton, was a big deal in Washington, the number two man in the Department of Agriculture. Milton had married money, so he gave a lot of parties. Ike was at a party at Milton's one night, and he was leaving. And Milton turned to a reporter and said, "I want you to meet my brother before he goes. You ought to get to know him. He's going places."

And the reporter looked at this forty-five-year-old major as he shook his hand and thought, "If you're going places, you better get started soon." Well, that wasn't the way it worked in the old army. Eisenhower hung on. In 1939 he thought he was going to be forcibly retired as a lieutenant colonel.

Now, how did he rise so fast? Because in the army they knew talent when they saw it. Douglas MacArthur had written on Eisenhower's personnel report in 1927, "This is the best officer in the United States Army. When the next war comes, move him right to the top." And he had that reputation throughout the army. He told his son John, "My ambition has always been to do so well at my job that whenever I'm transferred, my superior is going to regret my leaving."

When war comes, it opens up opportunities, especially for professional officers. And Eisenhower did well at every posting that he got. Marshall had been so impressed by him that he had sent him over to London — and Ike was just a temporary, one-star general at this time, and there were dozens and hundreds of them in the army as it expanded. But he was the one that Marshall picked to send over to London and give a recommendation on how to set up a headquarters there.

And Ike came back and said to Marshall, "The number one thing is to give absolute control to a supreme commander. We've got to have one boss." And Marshall replied, "You're satisfied with this report you've given and the steps that you've recommended that we take to create such a command?" And Ike said, "Yes, I'm satisfied, I'll stand behind them." And Marshall said, "Good, because you're going to implement it."

And then he was off and running. He had the most coveted command. Now, at the time, Marshall didn't think that it was going to necessarily be a field command. Marshall thought Eisenhower would be there as his deputy, building up the forces that he, Marshall, would come to command for the great invasion of France in 1943. Well, none of that worked out.

Q: Why?

A: Roosevelt and Churchill's insistence on a '42 invasion meant that Eisenhower got that first command in North Africa, and he did well enough that he survived — and it's very rare in a big war for a general to survive that first major campaign. Eisenhower got through that North Africa thing. And, from then on, it was right on to the top.

A major factor in that was how well the British liked him, which wasn't the case with men like Mark Clark, who was a rival, or George Patton, or certainly Douglas MacArthur. The British couldn't abide any of those guys.

Q: Why not?

A: Oh, they were so anti-British, they were so American, they never could see a British point of view. They were the American equivalent of Montgomery on the British side, who couldn't abide Americans. And it hurt Montgomery badly.

Q: So, what was it about Ike that they liked?

A: Him. Listen, Roger, this is the best man that this

country produced in this century—the most honest, the most trustworthy, the hardest-working, the most ambitious, the most decisive, the one who thought problems through better than anybody else, the best politician, and on and on and on. I mean, and the Brits recognized all this right away, Churchill took one look at Eisenhower, had one evening with him, and had fallen in love.

And Eisenhower tried to stay aloof from Churchill, which was very hard to do. When Churchill put the arms around someone, it took an awful lot to resist. Ike wasn't altogether successful in resisting Churchill's charms, but, on Churchill's part, he just thought Eisenhower was terrific.

Q: What was Eisenhower's relationship with Douglas MacArthur? Was it a difficult one or not?

A: Very difficult, volatile. MacArthur—this sounds terrible, but it's true—MacArthur lied his way out of every difficulty he ever got into. And Eisenhower was under him as his chief of staff for many years in the Philippines and, before that, in Washington. So Eisenhower had to put up with this behavior. Now, that was just the way MacArthur was, and there are innumerable examples of it. But Eisenhower was the one who had to live through it. On the other hand, for all of these criticisms of MacArthur—which Ike confined to his diary, which is pretty explosive—he did stay with him and work with him all of that time. He wrote MacArthur's speeches for him; he did all of the dirty work.

Here's something that illustrates the relationship: MacArthur got a big idea. He decided to have a parade in Manila to show the Filipino people this wonderful army that he was building for them. And he told Ike to get on it. But Lieutenant Colonel Eisenhower protested. He said, "General, that's a terrible idea. It'll interrupt training, it'll cost us about a year's budget to bring everybody in from all the outlying islands to Manila. We'll have to build barracks in Manila for them. I mean, the cost of this thing doesn't begin to justify having a parade." MacArthur said, "Do it." So, Eisenhower got started on doing it.

And the president of the commonwealth, Manuel Quezon, called Ike, and said, "What the hell's going on? I see all these troop movements going on and these barracks being built and this money being spent. What's happening?" And Eisenhower said, "You'll have to talk to MacArthur." Quezon called MacArthur, still agitated, "What the hell's going on here?" MacArthur said, "I don't know anything about it. That's Lieutenant Colonel Eisenhower's project. He's the one. Talk to him."

Can you imagine? Pretty hard to put up with that as a subordinate over a very long period of time. But Ike did put up with it, and he learned quite a lot from MacArthur. He learned how to see things from the high command's point of view. He also learned a lot of negatives from MacArthur, far more than the positives. Eisenhower once said, "I studied dramatics under MacArthur for nine years."

Q: I know that quote, but I always thought it was apocryphal.

A: No, it's true.

Q: Is it also true that Eisenhower was made

commander in chief of the Allied Expeditionary Force almost by default?

A: Well, in a way. Roosevelt had to make the decision quickly because Stalin put a gun to his head. At the Teheran conference in 1943, Roosevelt had assured Stalin, "We're going in 1944, there's going to be an invasion. We're going to finally have that second front that we've been promising." And Stalin said, "Who's going to command it?" When Roosevelt told him that hadn't been decided on yet, Stalin said, "Then I don't believe you. I think you're up to your old tricks."

So, Roosevelt got back to Cairo from Teheran, having to make the decision. Now, he wanted Marshall to have the job. Most people in the army wanted Marshall to have the job, and, obviously, Marshall wanted to have the job. He had built this army for exactly this invasion and, of course, he wanted to command it.

But then Roosevelt began to have second thoughts. So he thought, "I'll leave it up to General Marshall. I respect him more than any other living person. I'll let him decide." And he asked Marshall, "What do you want to do? What do you think?" Marshall said, "Mr. President, that's your decision. You've got to decide where I can best serve you, period."

Roosevelt thought about it some more, and then, as he put it, "I just decided I couldn't sleep at night with General Marshall out of Washington." Now, the deal they were going to cut was this: Marshall would go to London and take command of Operation Overlord, and Eisenhower would come back and replace him as chief of staff. Well, that made no sense. You couldn't make Eisenhower Marshall's boss, and you certainly couldn't make Eisenhower MacArthur's boss. So, the quote "I couldn't sleep at night with General Marshall out of the country" really meant, "We've got to keep Marshall as chief of staff to handle MacArthur." So, in that sense, Ike got it by default.

But in the positive sense, he got it because he had done well in North Africa, he had done well in Sicily, he had done well in Italy, he was getting along famously with the British, he knew all the commanders that were in the field there. It was almost as if it was fate that he had been brought to this moment, through that long apprenticeship in the army, then the North African invasion, and then the Mediterranean campaign. He was primed for what was the most coveted command in history.

And these guys knew, if this one succeeds, the commander can do whatever he wants.

Q: You think his appointment as the commander in chief made his nomination as president inevitable?

A: Well, he had to succeed first. After he succeeded, yeah, it was inevitable that there would be a groundswell for the most successful and popular general of the war—just as there had been for Grant and for Sherman, too, of course, who turned it down. And remember, Eisenhower turned the opportunity down in 1948. He could have had either party's nomination in 1948. Harry Truman told him, "I'll run as number two on the ticket if you'll head up the Democratic effort in 1948."

Q: That's hard to believe.

A: Isn't it? Ike said, "You know I'm not a Democrat." As it turned out, Harry Truman and Ike's oldest brother, Arthur Eisenhower, had been roommates in Kansas City at the turn of the century. The Truman family knew the Eisenhower family. So Truman knew Ike's politics. And Ike told him, "You know I'm a Republican. I'm not going to run for the Democratic Party."

Q: I read carefully your descriptions of Eisenhower, and you said that he was "a competent soldier who was well-versed," but you didn't say he was brilliant or that he was masterful. I keep wondering whether that's not faint praise.

A: Well, it's not intended as faint praise. Eisenhower was competent to the job. Professionally, he knew the army, he knew their boots, he knew their weapons, he'd handled every one of the weapons. He knew the organization of the army. He knew the individuals in the army. He knew all the guys in the high command of the army personally.

These were professional attributes that he had to have to succeed in his job. But he had to have a lot more, too. He had to be able to get the British to get along with the Americans. He had to bring the French in on this, and then to deal with Charles de Gaulle. He had to be a diplomat as well as a warrior. And in that role, he shone. There was nobody to touch him.

But then people do try to almost denigrate Eisenhower by saying, "Well, he had that big grin, and he was so friendly, and he obviously loved people. So, of course, people liked him and he got people to get along together and that was his talent." Yeah, that was a part of the talent. But there was more to it than that. There was a decisiveness and a hardness to Eisenhower that showed best on his decision on June 5, 1944: "OK, let's go." Now, he was throwing two hundred thousand young men into the Atlantic wall. He was making a decision that affected not only their lives and the lives of the German boys on the other side, but the fate of great nations was at stake here.

When he made that decision, he was pacing. He had his chin down and his hands behind his back and was pacing, as he did when he was in deep thought. He had talked to his weatherman, who had said, "I think this storm is going to break, but you better know, General, that my opposite number in the American forces"—he had a British weatherman—"doesn't agree with me."

And then Eisenhower polled fourteen men in the room, his immediate subordinates—Montgomery and Bradley and the rest. It wasn't a vote. He just wanted to know their views from the point of view of their own specialty—air, sea, ground. The ground guys all wanted to go, the sea guys were very hesitant, the air guys didn't want to go at all. So, they split seven to seven.

And Eisenhower had to decide. If he postponed, he was going to have to postpone for two weeks, because of the tide and moon requirements of the invasion. Bedell Smith, Ike's chief of staff, said it best: "Watching Eisenhower pacing up there, I was struck by the loneliness and isolation of high command." And it has always seemed to me to be the perfect description of Eisenhower. As a general and as president, he knew that loneliness and he knew that isolation, and he never shrank from them.

Q: After he made the decision to go, did he sleep well that night?

A: He slept as well as he did any night. He got through the war on four hours of sleep a night, twenty cups of coffee a day, and four packs of Camel cigarettes, and an occasional sandwich. That's how he got through the war. But he made that decision, and then he went out and visited with the troops that were loading up. It was four o'clock in the morning when he made that decision, and he went out to the airfield to watch as the Eighty-second was about to take off. And he circulated. Some of the most famous pictures of Ike in the war resulted from that.

Q: "Anybody here from Kansas?" That was the great line.

A: Yeah. He asked, "Anybody here from Kansas?" And this kid said, "I'm from Kansas, sir, I'm from Topeka, very proud." And Ike said, "Well, son, what's your name?" His name was Sherman Oyler. I've met him. But Oyler was so dumbstruck by being addressed directly by God himself, he forgot his name.

In one of my favorite scenes, Eisenhower was telling these guys, "Don't worry, we've got a good plan. You've got tremendous follow-up forces coming behind you. We're going to surprise them. Just get in there and do your job and don't worry." And one kid piped up, saying, "General, hell, we ain't worried. It's Hitler's turn to worry now."

Another of my favorite scenes from that June 5th occurred at the end of the day, when the Eighty-second was taking off from the airfield, and Ike was out there—I got this story from Ike himself. And the last guy to get on a plane, he said, was just a little kid—five foot three, five foot four—I don't know how the hell he ever got into the paratroopers. There was more equipment than there was man. He had to be helped up into the plane. And he got into the C-47, and just before they closed the door, he turned and snapped out a salute to Ike, which Ike returned. Then the kid turned to the east and he said, "Look out, Hitler, here we come."

Q: What did Hitler think of the American soldier, Dr. Ambrose?

A: Hitler was contemptuous of the Americans. There was a precedent for that. So was Erich Ludendorff, who was head of the German military, an almost dictator of Germany in World War I. When Ludendorff instituted unrestricted submarine warfare in January of 1917, his people said, "This is going to bring America into the war." And Ludendorff replied, "They can't fight. It's a race of mongrels." And Hitler had exactly that view. Hitler was certain that the kids that he had brought up in the Hitler Youth would always outfight the Boy Scouts. He thought of the American soldier as the spoiled son of democracy who would never be able to withstand the rigors of the modern battlefield. Hitler made a mistake.

Q: Why do you think the American soldier fought as well as he did? I mean, all those armies were citizen armies.

A: Sure, of course, they were all mass armies, that's

right. You had a stronger cadre of professionals in the British army, in the French army, in the German army, even in the Red Army, although Stalin had managed to kill most of his colonels and generals. But there was more of a professional core to those armies than there was to the American army.

The American army went from 160,000 men in 1940 to 8 million men by 1945. That's some expansion. Well, they did well. And, indeed, by the fall of 1944, they were the best army in the world. Now, partly, this was because in many areas they had the best equipment. Now, this wasn't always the case. Their cannon weren't as good as German cannon. The German jet aircraft was way superior to anything we put into the air, although the Germans didn't get very many of them into the air.

But, generally, the Americans had awfully good equipment, especially the trucks and the Jeeps and the landing craft. And in these areas, they had a mobility that all other armies through history can only envy — even in 1990. Ike could move troops around Europe faster than we could move troops to the Gulf in 1990. So, they had this tremendous mobility, and they had good weaponry. They also had good, competent, professional leaders at the very top — Eisenhower, Bradley, and so forth. But the rest were citizen soldiers. This goes for all the junior officers, too. West Point couldn't begin to fill the demand. And all the noncommissioned officers. Those old army NCOs didn't make it past 1942.

Q: Wiped out.

A: They were wiped out, yeah. This was too big a war for them.

Then, at the heart, the Americans had good training. They were the children of democracy and they were Boy Scouts. They had learned to take responsibility. They had learned to take an initiative. On that point, for example, the distinction between the various armies couldn't be sharper. Rommel did not have a suggestion box outside his door. Eisenhower did; Bradley did.

When Americans got into the hedgerows, in June of 1944, it was completely unexpected—a terrible breakdown of American intelligence. The problem was, those hedgerows were about six feet tall, with a lot of bramble and trees growing over them. A tank would come into the hedgerow and go belly-up as it tried to climb out of it. Then a German eighteen-year-old could shoot right into the belly of that tank. What the hell to do about this completely unanticipated problem?

What happened was that a cabdriver from Chicago, who was a tank driver in the Second Armored Regiment, said, "Let's take these steel rails that Rommel used to make the defenses at the beach"—he had Teller mines on top of them, and if a landing craft came in, it would hit it and explode—"let's take those rails and weld them on to the front of the tank, and then the tank will dig into that hedgerow.

"And with the power of the Chrysler engine, it can go right on through the damn thing, and then you can start spraying the corners of the hedgerow." These were little tiny fields, and they could "spray the corners," where the Germans set up their machine guns, "with the 50 cal and start hitting them with those 75 cannon on those Sherman tanks, and we'll get through that hedgerow."

Well, this cabdriver's name was Sergeant Joe Cullen from Chicago. Cullen made this suggestion on a Tuesday morning. By Tuesday night, it was on Bradley's desk, and by Wednesday morning, they were starting to do it. That didn't happen in other armies.

The American kids had great mechanical ability. There was hardly a kid in that army who hadn't taken apart and put back together an internal combustion engine. When an American tank got blasted, they didn't do like the Russians or the Germans did—or the British, come to that—which was just abandon the damn thing. They stripped it. There were a lot of good spark plugs still left on that tank. There was good tread left on the far side of the tank, and so forth. I mean, these kids were taking the skills they had learned as mechanics back in the States and applying them in the army.

There was also an ingenuity to the American GI that was lacking in other armies. And I'm convinced this came out of being a participating member of a free society. Hitler thought totalitarianism is by far the most efficient form of government. With the squabbling of the parliamentarians, Hitler was just contemptuous of the French and the British—and at least in the French case, it turned out he was right to be contemptuous. But he was equally contemptuous of the Americans. The Americans, of course, were very slow to rise to the challenge. But as Eisenhower wrote to his brother Milton on September 1, 1939, the day the war began: "Hitler should beware the fury of an aroused democracy." Well, the U.S. Army of World War II became the tip of the spear of that aroused democracy. And we just did wonderfully well.

Q: Was there much cowardice in the U.S. Army?

A: Sure. Of course.

Q: What did they do about it?

A: They did what all armies do about it: try to punish, try to set an example, try to talk to the kid, try to help him out.

Q: Did they shoot any of them?

A: Ike had had one shot. His name was Eddie Slovik. He was from Pennsylvania.

Q: Famous case.

A: Famous case. Eddie came over in the fall of '44 as a replacement. He deserted immediately. And he hooked up with a Canadian unit and hid out with them for about six weeks. Then they turned him in. And he told the officer who was taking him back, "If you send me back to the front line, I'm going to run away again, I promise you. I can't take it. I'm not going to be up there. You're going to have to court-martial me."

Now, what Eddie wanted was go to prison, go to the stockade. These guys all knew there would be a blanket amnesty when the war was over. And much better to spend the winter of '44–'45 in the stockade than at Bastogne. So, Eddie really challenged him.

There were, I think, 149 cases of desertion that were brought all the way to trial and then to a judgment of guilty and death by the firing squad. That had not been done since 1864. Of those 149, Eisenhower approved one sentence, and it was Eddie Slovik's, because he had just challenged them to so directly. Eddie was also very un-lucky in his timing, because by the time his case came before Eisenhower for final review, we were in the mid-dle of the Battle of the Bulge. And there were desertions in the Battle of the Bulge—guys that ran away from the lines.

Of course, it was fairly easy to desert in Europe, a hell of a lot easier than it was in the Pacific, because you looked like the people on the streets.

Q: You weren't on an island, either.

A: Right, exactly. So, Eisenhower approved Eddie's execution, and it was carried out. He was very widely criticized for that and still is. The act needs to be put into a certain perspective. That's one man in an eleven-month campaign that Eisenhower had executed for de-sertion and cowardice. And that same time, on that same front, Hitler had fifty thousand executed. So, Hitler ran his army through terror.

Now, obviously, the Germans had awfully good sol-diers. The Russians made great soldiers. The Japanese had some good soldiers. But there were certain qualities to the U.S. Army that go beyond the material, that made it so special. And the most important of these was "I don't want to ever be in a position in which I have let my buddies down."

They weren't staying in those front lines in those awful conditions because of Mom and apple pie and American democracy. They were staying there because they knew, "If I leave my position, that's going to endan-ger Harry over there on the right and Joe over there, and I'm not going to do that. I'll do anything to get out of here, except let my buddies down."

Of course, they meant it when they said they would do anything to get out of there. That's summed up in the phrase, "A million-dollar wound." People hear that phrase and they think, "Well, it's a shot through the muscle of the arm, and then you get to go home." No. It didn't work like that. They'd patch you up in two weeks on a wound like that and have you back in the front lines. The only way you could get out of there was to lose a limb. That was a million-dollar wound.

My most vivid image of the Battle of the Bulge is an American kid in a foxhole, who had his left hand blown off by a passing 88 shell. It just took the hand away. And the blood started to spurt out. This kid gets out of the foxhole, holding his stump up in the air with the blood going out onto the snow of Belgium, and he ran around the foxhole shouting out to his buddies, "Thank you, God, thank you, I'm going home."

Q: Horrible.

A: That's how bad it was there. But they stuck it out. And they stuck it out because of unit cohesion and because of their relationship with their buddies.

Now, the Americans had a terrible replacement policy, because it brought kids forward as individuals. It didn't bring them in with the squad, the platoon, the company they had trained in. So, they were getting thrown into the line as individual replacements. My number one criticism of Eisenhower in World War II is that he let this system go forward. If the replacements came in as individuals, that meant they didn't know the name of the guy to the left and to the right. It meant they hadn't gotten drunk with them, they hadn't had their first sexual experience in a bordello with these guys, they hadn't hated the same drill sergeant together. All the things that go into bringing men together in the army, they didn't have any of it.

Q: So there was no unit cohesion?

A: There was no unit cohesion at all. And those replacements suffered terribly as a result. But, overall, the Americans developed a bond, as did other armies. The German army was especially good at getting squads together. They did it in a way that our National Guard units tried to emulate. The Germans tried to make a squad out of kids from the same village, and then a platoon from the same region, or a company, so that they had known each other all their lives. And the National Guard units in the U.S. Army in World War II were somewhat like that.

Q: I know another thing that sticks in your craw about the U.S. Army is the prevalence of trench foot. Somewhere in your book, you say that trench foot wiped out the equivalent of three divisions?

A: Forty-five thousand men. Three rifle divisions.

Q: What is trench foot?

A: Well, it comes with cold and wet between your toes and spreads. It's athlete's foot run amok. They got it because the army had issued leather boots, and they were wearing leather boots in those Belgian foxholes, when it was going down to zero at night, and got up to about forty degrees in the daytime. So they were standing in water and then on ice. These leather boots soaked up that water and these guys were getting trench foot, just terrible.

The crime here was that they had good winter boots available, the kind that L. L. Bean made popular after the war, with the big rubber and then the leather and the padding and all. But those were all gobbled up by the rear echelon. Every GI in Paris in services supplies was wearing those boots by December, all of the quartermasters were, the truck drivers were, the guys unloading the ships were. Everybody in the rear echelon had those boots.

Q: How did that happen?

A: They had to make their way from the higher-ups to the front line, and guys grabbed a pair here, grabbed a pair there. Just like Lucky Strikes. The army gave free cigarettes to the troops in World War II. The ones they wanted most were Lucky Strikes, second were Camels. Well, the Lucky Strikes and Camels never made it past Paris. And what they got up in the front lines were Raleighs.

Q: Now, what actually happened with trench foot?

A: Well, first the toes would get so bad that you couldn't walk. I've interviewed company commanders who had their men being carried up to their foxholes to their firing positions. Then it would spread. In a bad case, they had to amputate the toes. In a really bad case, they had to amputate the foot. And, in some cases, it got all the way up to the knee.

Q: It became gangrene?

A: Yeah. So, it was just a debilitating, god-awful thing to have. Now, the army took the view that a lot of guys were getting this deliberately, but it was just absurd of the army to come to such a conclusion. Nobody would do that to themselves deliberately, when they always had the alternative of shooting themselves in the foot. And that did happen. There were men who did that. It was almost impossible to prove that it hadn't been an accident. They had to evacuate you. That meant you got clean sheets that night. You got warmth. You got hot food. You got American nurses taking care of you. And nobody was shooting at you. And you'd get a month, a month and a half off from the line, and maybe, by then, the war would be over.

Those were long, terrible nights in those foxholes. I've talked to veterans' groups, and I've never once had a man tell me that I'm wrong when I say, "Everybody in those foxholes had to have that thought during those nights: 'God, one quick shot in the foot and I'm out of here.'" So, what impresses me is not that there were a few hundred who did it, but there were tens of thousands who didn't.

Q: Do you think the average GI knew what was at stake in this war?

A: One of my all-time favorite quotations from a GI came at the conclusion of an interview I was conducting, and I basically asked him what you just asked me. He answered, "Steve, I was nineteen years old. I had my life ahead of me. I knew the difference between right and wrong, and I didn't want to grow up in a world in which wrong prevailed."

Q: What do you think was at stake?

A: In World War II? Western civilization, nothing short of it. The future of democracy. We went into the twentieth century with competing ideologies. The autocracies fought against the democracies in the First World War, and they lost. Then here came the Fascists and the Communists, and now you had this titanic struggle going on between Fascists, Communists, and the democracies. And I'll tell you what: In 1940, '41, it looked terrible for the democracies; it looked like they were done, for sure. Either the Communists or the Nazis were going to triumph in this war.

By 1944, it was questionable. The democracies had made an awful big comeback, primarily the United States, of course, and had begun to build armed forces that could take on these totalitarian armies. But it was a damn close run thing.

Q: You don't think it was inevitable that the Allies would win?

A: Of course not. Absolutely not. Nothing is inevitable in life. That's my most basic position as historian: People make choices, and those choices have results, and we all live with the results. Now, in December of 1941 the people of the United States made a choice, and they made it prevail. They turned this century on its head. In 1945, it was impossible to believe in that nineteenth-century concept of progress that had driven the nineteenth century—the notion that every day, in every way, we're getting better and better.

And that was almost universally believed in the Western world. And then came World War I. Then came World War II, climaxing with the atomic bomb. And it seemed like we had been betrayed. Exactly those forces that we had looked to to make life better and better— science and technology—had given us the ability to destroy the whole world. And what was there in 1945 to make anybody think that that wasn't going to happen?

World War III seemed inevitable when I was in high school, right after the war. These GIs that had fought to defeat Hitler and Tojo provided the basis for an American policy that we were going to wait these guys out. But we were not going to engage in any nuclear warfare; we were not going to destroy the world. We were not going to give it up, either. We were going to stand up.

Now, this is entirely different from our approach to Hitler. The approach to Hitler was "We've got to crush him." After the war, Hitler was crushed. Now here comes Stalin, doing things in Poland that were just terrible. It'd be awfully hard to choose who is worse, Hitler or Stalin, in command in Poland and Hungary and elsewhere.

Our first instinct was "Let's go after Stalin the way we went after Hitler—and we've got the power to do it." But that generation said, "No." They followed Eisenhower's lead on this, and before Eisenhower, it was Harry Truman who established a policy of containment, of course. Containment was based on a notion that

Eisenhower expressed best to a group of congressmen who had come in to urge him to make a first strike against the Soviet Union in 1957. They said, "We can destroy them, boss, and they can't retaliate. And, otherwise, we're going to be having to pay out these outrageous costs for defense for a very long time to come." And Eisenhower said, "That's right, this is not a short-run thing here. This is going to take a very long time. But if the Soviets want to keep up with us, and they do, they're going to have to educate their own people. And in the process, they will sow the seeds of their own destruction." And that's almost a one-sentence summary of what finally led to *glasnost* and *perestroika,* which inevitably led to the collapse of the Soviet Union.

So now, at the end of the twentieth century, we now live in a time in which it is possible to once again believe in progress. It is possible to believe that things are going to get better. There's no reason not to think so, because we survived the last sixty years of the twentieth century, 1940 to the end of the Cold War.

After I finished an interview with one of the GIs, I asked him the kind of general question you do at the end of an interview: "Well, what do you think? Was it worth it?" He said, "Listen, I feel like I've played my part in turning this from a century of darkness into a century of light." That's nice. That's a nice way to put it.

Q: I wanted to ask you about the GI as an occupying soldier. After that first six months, when we broke through and crossed the Rhine, we were mainly occupying Germany.

A: Germany and Austria, that's right.

Q: So, what kind of occupying troops were the American soldiers?

A: Let me start off by saying this: The spring of 1945 was the worst spring the world has ever known. More people were killed violently in 1945 than any other year in the world's history. And at that time, around the world, the sight of twelve teenage boys in uniform, carrying rifles, brought terror to people's hearts. It didn't matter whether they were Russian boys in Berlin or Leipzig or Kraków or Warsaw, or German boys, who still occupied Holland, or Japanese boys in Manila or Seoul or Canton—because the sight of twelve teenage armed boys meant rape, pillage, looting, senseless destruction, and wanton murder.

But there was an exception, and that exception was a squad of American GIs. Those twelve armed young men stood for something else; they meant candy, cigarettes, and C-rations—and freedom. And you can expand the image of that little squad around the world. We had sent our best young men halfway around the world in both directions, not to conquer, not to terrorize, but to liberate. And not just to liberate our allies, but also to liberate our foes. We liberated the Germans as much as we liberated the French. We liberated the Japanese from one of the most criminal, god-awful governments the world has ever known. It was a great moment in American history.

That's what my wife means by "triumphalism," by the way.

Q: When you look back at D-day, you must regard D-day as the linchpin of the twentieth century.

A: It was the pivot point. There's some hyperbole involved in that, of course. But an awful lot that had gone before in the twentieth century led up to D-day. And then, for sure, everything that has followed has been a consequence of D-day. Now, that's hyperbolic, because there were big battles yet to fight. But those battles wouldn't have been fought if we hadn't gotten ashore on D-day. If we hadn't gotten ashore on D-day, think of what the consequences would have been.

This was the supreme military effort of the Allies in the Second World War—D-day. What would have happened to the Churchill government if it had failed? It would have been out of power. Roosevelt was facing an election—already controversial because it was a fourth term—in November of 1944. If D-day had failed, there's no way in the world Roosevelt would have won that election. Then Churchill's successor and Roosevelt's successor would have been hard-pressed to do one of two things—either make a bigger effort, which was scarcely possible, or find some accommodation with the enemy. And the same applies in spades to Joe Stalin. If he saw that invasion fail, it would have taken months to prepare another one. Hitler could have transferred armored divisions, his Panzers, over to the eastern front. Stalin was looking at this, and if it failed, Stalin would have said to himself, "Maybe I better cut a deal with my dear friend Adolf again, because I can't rely on those guys, and I can't defeat Germany by myself."

And then you take off from there. Who knows in what directions world history would have gone?

Q: Now, to leap ahead, as we must: The war is over; Eisenhower comes home with the great parades and adulation. Then, as I read your biography, he sort of fell in with America's millionaires. Did he fall in willingly or did they come and sort of capture him?

A: Oh, they came to him.

Q: Why did they want him?

A: Because he was who he was, because he was the most successful general of the war, the most popular general of the war, and because he was the best man they'd ever met, any of them. When Eisenhower was president, the charge was that he'd sold out to America's corporate interests and to the millionaires. But it wasn't that way at all. They sold out to him.

Q: What do you mean by that?

A: Well, Eisenhower was able to take some of these men—these fabulously rich, very far-right-wing guys—and lead them into the modern world. H. L. Hunt from Texas was one example. They would listen to him in a way they wouldn't listen to others. For example, when he said to them, "We've got to support these European governments," and they said, "What the hell are you talking about? They're all socialists." Ike said, "You've got to understand that socialism means something different over in Europe, and as long as they're democratic, they're on our side. I don't care if they're socialists or not, and you guys need to get onto this train, because it's leaving the station."

He was able to persuade prewar isolationists, men of great prestige and power and wealth, that, "Yes, we've got to support democracies. I don't care if they've got a Labor government in Britain or not, I don't care if they're nationalizing their coal mines and the railroads. It's a democratic nation, and they're our friends, and they're our allies, and they're the people we've got to stick with." And he was able to persuade these guys of that.

Q: Were those millionaires the ones who, in fact, set him up for the presidency?

A: Well, there was a lot of push to get him into the presidency from—even in 1944, there were columnists talking about how he ought to be running for president. The pressure became very great in 1948. As I said, both parties wanted to nominate him.

And he took the very high ground, saying that soldiers ought not to be involved in politics. He made a Sherman-like statement: "Forget about me. If you nominate me, I'm not going to run; and I'm not going to serve if you elect me." He didn't put it quite as strongly as Sherman did, but almost that strongly.

If he had died in 1950, Eisenhower would be remembered today as the only man, along with William T. Sherman, to turn down the presidency of the United States. He was convinced to run in 1952, by the millionaires and professional politicians, and his own brother Milton, who said, "If you don't run, it's going to be the end of the Republican Party."

Eisenhower recognized that. In fact, on election night, 1948, he told his son John, "This is the worst night of my life, because Dewey got beat." Eisenhower thought that Dewey would win and then serve a second term. Then it would be 1956. By that time, he thought, he'd be too old to be president, and all this pressure would be off of him. As soon as Dewey lost, Ike knew that he was trapped. He tried to escape, but by '52, they were able to convince him. They convinced him by using the key word with Eisenhower—they convinced him he had a "duty." He had a duty to the American people and the American political system to run: "Only you can save us." And he was convinced by that. "If you don't run, it's the end of the Republican Party." I think that that was a gross exaggeration.

Q: Robert Taft would have been the nominee.

A: Taft would have been the nominee and he would've been slaughtered by Truman. My view is that Truman would have run again, and it was Eisenhower's announcement that he was going to become a candidate, at the end of 1951, that made Truman decide, "Well, I'm getting out. I'm not going to run against Eisenhower."

Q: So did Eisenhower save us?

A: As I say, I think it was pretty much a gross exaggeration. I think the Republic would have survived an Adlai Stevenson presidency or a Bob Taft presidency. The great danger without Eisenhower would have been a nuclear war. The pressure was so great to make that first strike, because we had such a big lead and because the Soviets were so antagonistic and impossible to deal with. They were doing terrible things in Eastern Europe and in Central Europe and in Asia, so the temptation was very great.

And many times—on at least four separate occasions during Eisenhower's presidency—the secretary of state, John Foster Dulles, the vice president, Richard Nixon, and the joint chiefs of staff came into the Oval Office and said, "We ought to do it now, right now." And Eisenhower said, "No, we're not going to do that." I think in the 1950s, Eisenhower was the only man who could have gotten away with that. I don't think Adlai Stevenson could have stood up to that kind of pressure.

But in Eisenhower's case, as one senator, who was very hawkish, remarked, "How can I argue with Eisenhower on military matters?" There were times in the 1950s when Eisenhower was the only man holding down the cost of defense, saying, "No, we don't need this, we don't need that, we've got a big enough lead. We need to deter. We're not out to destroy. We're going to keep the lid on it."

Again, I don't think anybody else could have done that.

Q: But you'd think it would be the other way with a military man, wouldn't you?

A: Except Eisenhower.

Q: Well, what do you mean, "Except Eisenhower"?

A: Well, let me make clear—my admiration and love for the man is unbounded. I've got a lot of criticisms of him, and I make them, but, overall, he was just Ike. He was so much more than a soldier. He was a great soldier. But he was a great human being beyond that.

And the chiefs said to him, "Let's do it now." He answered, "Listen, guys: What do you suppose will happen next? Here you'll have this vast area, all the way from the Elbe River to Vladivostok, just nothing but destruction—no communications, no hospitals, just starvation and misery and death and disease. That's not a victory."

That's pretty good. I mean, I like that our president said that and felt that way. In fact, all of the presidents did, because they all had the temptation. But none stronger than Eisenhower, because that's when our lead was the biggest, in the 1950s.

Q: You said he was a great general, a great human being, and how do you classify him as a president?

A: Well, my own view is he was the best president of the twentieth century, but I don't say that publicly, because nobody's going to accept that.

Q: You just said it.

A: Well, none of the Roosevelt admirers are going to accept that—Teddy or Franklin. Not many fellow historians will accept it.

But in my view, he got us through the worst decade of the Cold War, without losing an inch of ground, without having a single soldier killed after July, when he got the armistice in Korea, and without having to destroy the Soviet Union. You look back on it now and think about these guys recommending that kind of a first strike. Can you imagine how awful that would have been? How ashamed you would be to be an American? And Eisenhower was the one who prevented it.

Also, remember, the '50s were a fabulous decade. We had 4 percent real growth every year, with a 1 percent, or a 1.2 percent, inflation rate through those eight years. This was an accomplishment. A lot of it was luck; a lot of it was being there at the time that a lot of this was going to happen anyway. But a lot of it was due to Eisenhower. He was a great builder. He built the interstate highway system, he built the St. Lawrence Seaway. He was a great steward. He vastly expanded the National Park and the National Forest Service.

There were things that were wrong, of course, and they speak to Eisenhower's character and personality. After all, the '50s was the best decade of this century if you were white, male, and middle class. Those years weren't good for blacks. In fact, it was a pretty bad decade for blacks. It wasn't all that good a decade for women. In fact, it was a pretty bad decade for women. Those were problems that Eisenhower refused to face, not out of cowardice and not due to political motives, judging by what the polls have got to say. Eisenhower was born six years before *Plessy* v. *Ferguson* was handed down. Eisenhower thought segregation was the right way for the races to relate to each other. He just was a Victorian on that, period. He was a Victorian on Jews. And he had no Jewish friends. He was not a great friend of Israel. And, of course, in 1956, he made the Israelis get out of Suez. And he was not a great friend of women. I mean, his idea of the proper women's role was as a mother or secretary. These were the limitations of his time and place and his upbringing, as well as his character and his personality.

Q: Was he also a great friend of Senator Joseph McCarthy?

A: Yes, that's another place where he fell short. He refused to stand up to him. The closest he came was at a Dartmouth commencement speech, when he said, "Don't join the book burners," without naming McCarthy by name. And that was taken to be a severe rebuke of Joe McCarthy. Eisenhower had it in his power to make McCarthy stop his nonsense, and he didn't do it. And he needs to be faulted for that.

There is a famous incident that happened in Milwaukee in the campaign in 1952, when Eisenhower deleted a paragraph of praise of General Marshall from his speech. He had wanted to deliver the speech with McCarthy on the platform, as a rebuke to McCarthy for calling General Marshall, of all things, "a traitor." But Eisenhower was persuaded by Governor Walter Kohler of Wisconsin to take the paragraph out. Kohler said, "We've got to carry Wisconsin. Harry Truman carried the state in 1948, and if you rebuke Senator McCarthy on his home turf, that won't happen. Go say it somewhere else, General, but just don't say it in Milwaukee." That's politics.

So Ike yanked the paragraph out. The problem was that the advance copies had already gotten out to the press, and Eisenhower's aides were telling the press, who were pushing on Eisenhower to say something about McCarthy: "Wait till you hear what he says in Milwaukee, and then you'll find out what the general really believes about Joe McCarthy." And then they heard the speech, and he had taken the paragraph out. That was the one moment in his life I never dared talk to him about.

Q: Why?

A: Because he was so embarrassed by it. He tried not to put it into his memoirs at all, but John Eisenhower, who was his aide on writing the memoirs, and his editors said, "General, you've got to say something about Joe McCarthy and George Marshall and the Milwaukee speech." And they had to drag him kicking and screaming into writing the most innocuous little paragraph. He was embarrassed by what he had done, and he ought to have been embarrassed by it.

Q: When you were doing the Eisenhower biography, what kind of schedule did you have?

A: I'd go to Gettysburg two or three times a week and spend the day with him. I'd talk to him, and ask him questions, and bring up his papers and say, "This is confusing to me," or, "Who is this guy Crawford that you're referring to here?" He was a wonderful guy to work with, because he gave you his total concentration. Now, it was characteristic of Eisenhower that he made eye contact. You look at any picture of Eisenhower during the war, and I guarantee you that he's going to be making eye contact with the soldier he's talking to. And that was just his way. He would fasten those blue eyes on you, and they never left. And he would concentrate on what you wanted to talk about.

He didn't fidget, he didn't change the subject. I was there for a purpose, he wanted to meet that purpose, and he would deal with what I was talking about.

One of my favorite memories is the time that we had been talking about Kasserine Pass, which was the defeat that he suffered in 1942, in his first battle in Africa. He had his jacket off, his tie down, and his sleeves rolled up. He was leaning over on the map, and talking the way he talked, which was with an awful lot of curse words. I mean, he was a professional soldier, and that's the way he talked. There was a knock on the door, and his secretary said that, "The editors are here from Doubleday." This was for the presidential memoirs, which was pretty important stuff. But he said, "I want to talk to Dr. Ambrose some more."

And then the knock came again, and then the third time, he said, "All right." I started to gather up my maps and my notes and put them into my briefcase. And I watched as his shirtsleeves came down and the tie went up and the jacket went on, and he sat up, and here came the Doubleday editors to talk to him about the presidency. Just in front of my eyes, he had switched from being a general stuck in the mud of North Africa in 1942 to being president of the United States—and all the curse words disappeared.

Q: He called you "Dr. Ambrose"?

A: And I called him "General." He never told me that, but I felt he preferred that to being "Mr. President."

Q: One more question about the '50s: You said that

for the white, middle-class American male, the 1950s was the best decade. Why was it so good for them?

A: Well, real wages were going up 6 and 7 percent a year, with an inflation rate of 1 percent. Everybody had jobs. They were pouring out these new cars, the new television sets. Everybody was getting air conditioning. It was boom and prosperity around the country, again, if you were white and middle-class. But that didn't extend down into the ghettoes.

Q: But that's material. That's not spiritual, is it?

A: No, but that's usually what people vote on. As to spiritual, I come back to what we were talking about before. Eisenhower got us through without blowing up the Soviet Union, and you can't exaggerate how important that was, that he got us through the Cold War and had the confidence that we would prevail. "We're not going to go out there and slaughter those people." I think that's a moral decision that speaks to his spiritual qualities.

Q: Why did Dwight Eisenhower dislike Richard Nixon?

A: It's not quite fair to say he disliked him. He didn't like him.

Q: Did he trust him?

A: No, he didn't trust him. Nobody trusted Dick Nixon. Nixon wasn't looking for people to like him. And Nixon wasn't really looking for people to trust him. Nixon was looking for power. One of Eisenhower's most telling remarks about Nixon came a day after he had a conference with Nixon about the upcoming 1960 election. Nixon, of course, was going to be running against Kennedy. And Eisenhower told Ann Whitman, his secretary, as Nixon left the Oval Office, "I don't understand how a man can get through life without friends." Nixon didn't have friends; he didn't want friends. He had political associates.

Nixon had more acquaintances than anybody. I mean, Nixon could stand in a receiving line and he'd remember half the names in a crowd of a thousand, and he'd remember 250 of the guys' wives' names. And he'd remember an awful lot of the dogs' names. Nixon was a fabulous politician in that kind of a way. But he didn't have friends, and he didn't want friends. That, to me, is the biggest distinction between Eisenhower and Nixon. Eisenhower loved people; Nixon didn't.

Q: What kind of vice president was Nixon?

A: Oh, he was close to perfect, in that he did the things that Eisenhower wanted him to do.

Q: It's hard to be a bad vice president, I guess.

A: Well, I suppose it is. But it's hard to be a good one, too, much less a perfect one. But, anyway, Nixon served the role that he found himself in, that Eisenhower had created for him. He was the one that would get out after Adlai on the campaigns in '52 and in '56 and go around with those terrible Nixon hints that Adlai is a Communist or he's close to it, and so on—all the Communist-baiting that was so much a part of Nixon's career. Nixon was the guy who went out to the fund-raisers. Nixon flew around the world to the funerals. Nixon went down to Latin America on a goodwill tour. Nixon had a very good one with Khrushchev in the "kitchen debate" in Moscow at the American Exhibit in 1957. And Nixon delivered votes.

Nixon was the link to the right wing of the Republican Party, which was not at all happy with Eisenhower. Nixon provided that liaison. He didn't keep them happy, but he kept them quiet about their objections to some of the things that Eisenhower was doing. So, Nixon served him well as vice president.

Q: And, yet, as I read in your books, Eisenhower made a serious effort to prevent Nixon from getting the presidential nomination in 1960.

A: A major effort is putting it a little too strong. Let's go back to '56 first. In '56, Eisenhower did try very hard to get Nixon off the ticket. He had a list of names. But the party leaders convinced Eisenhower, "It's going to cost us three, four, five points, if we get Nixon off, and who have you got to substitute for him?" And so, Eisenhower kept Nixon—reluctantly, but he kept him.

Then, in 1960, he had a list that he made up—handwritten, it's in his papers—of his choices for his successor. Milton Eisenhower was first, but Ike thought, "We just can't do this."

Q: It wouldn't fly, would it?

A: It wouldn't fly, no. Robert Anderson, who was his secretary of the treasury, from Texas, was on that list. Alfred Gruenther, the general who had been the NATO commander, was on that list. Nixon was on the list, but I think he was twenty-third or twenty-fourth on the list. But Nixon had paid the dues, and every county chairman in the Republican Party in the United States had Dick Nixon down for a fund-raiser. And when the party spoke, it spoke decisively. I forget the figures, but something like three out of every four Republican congressmen signed a letter to Eisenhower, saying, "It's got to be Nixon. It's got to be Nixon."

Even then, Eisenhower wouldn't endorse Nixon before the nomination. He said, "I'm going to take a hands-off attitude. The party is a sovereign body, the party has the right to nominate whomever the party wants to nominate. Once the party has made a nomination, I'll get behind them." And Nixon said, "Boss, I'd like something a little earlier than that." But Ike didn't do it.

Q: I'm perplexed by your ability to take the measure of Eisenhower and your professed inability to take the measure of Nixon.

A: Well, Nixon's much more complex than Eisenhower.

Q: More complex?

A: Oh, yeah. Nixon is many-faceted. I think William Safire was the one who said that "Nixon is like those glass balls that have sharp angles on them, and they reflect." There is a new Nixon face for every situation. Nixon is Shakespearean. Only William Shakespeare could do an adequate biography of Dick Nixon. Those complexities just run so deep.

How do you explain this, for example? He was nominated five times by a major political party for national office—twice for vice president, and three times for president. He won four of those elections. And yet he thought he had been cheated by life. How do you explain a man who's so full of resentment, when he had been given such great talents? By God, he had marvelous parents; he grew up in California; he had an unbroken string of successes from the time he entered the navy right on through to Watergate. With the single exception of 1960, everything worked for Dick Nixon, but he was full of resentment and felt cheated by life. I don't know how to explain that. But I can tell you that that's the way he felt.

Q: Many politicians say publicly the opposite of what they've already decided privately, so that's not an exceptional quality. But reading your biography of Nixon, it's almost a hallmark of his style. How do you account for that? Is that duplicity or is it political savvy?

A: It's a combination of both, and of all the other things that went into the Nixon character. He just loved conspiracy. And he surrounded himself with people who loved conspiracy, beginning with Henry Kissinger and

H. R. Haldeman and John Ehrlichman and John Mitchell. I mean, what a bunch. They loved to spring surprises and say the opposite of what they were doing.

There's a kind of a civics point here, that Nixon and Kissinger were convinced that the only way to open to China was to do it secretly. So Kissinger made all that secret diplomacy. And there was never a national debate about whether we ought to open up to China or not. Nixon just sprang it on people. And he delighted in the surprise that he created by it.

Well, that was how he went about it. But there were other ways to go about it. First, you have a debate, as we did, for example, on the Marshall Plan. Harry Truman did not spring that on the country. We had a national debate on it. It was the same with joining NATO. That wasn't sprung on people. There was a national debate before it happened. And when you build a consensus through a national debate, you've got a lot more legs to a policy. And that's why the Truman policy of containment was to persist through all of his successors, right on to Bush and the end of the Cold War. That's why NATO has persisted, because we agreed as a people, "We want to do this."

We didn't agree as a people we wanted to open to China. Now, the opening to China had to be done. To praise Nixon for it is to ignore one fact: Who was the number one guy standing in the way of the recognition of China for twenty years? It was Dick Nixon. Nixon liked to say, "I'm the only guy who could've gotten it done." Of course he's the only guy who could've gotten it done, because he's the only guy that didn't have to deal with Dick Nixon as a critic. Can you imagine what Nixon would have said if Lyndon Johnson had tried to open to China? So, that was Nixon's way, to do it secretly.

He just loved that as much as he loved to rant and rave about things. Elliot Richardson once told me that he was sitting at a cabinet meeting, and Nixon said, "Oh, yeah, we've got to get rid of those goddamn Jews, and we've got to get all of these Harvards out of here and all these Ivy Leagues out of here, and I want to get some people in here that come from the midwestern universities. Goddamn it."

Richardson said, "I looked around the room and, of the fourteen cabinet members in the room, eight of us were Ivy League graduates and two of us were Jews." That was Nixon.

Q: Yet, you say that the greatest reelection victory in history—he carried forty-nine out of fifty states in 1972—was deserved.

A: Yeah, he was the better candidate.

Q: On the basis of what he had done in the first term?

A: That's right. Look, he had closed down the Vietnam War—or he almost had it closed down by the time of the election of 1972, and he had the American troops out of there. Now, it took him an agonizingly long time to do that, and there are many points along the way in which I think he made blunders and did things that were just stupid—Cambodian incursions come immediately to mind—but he got us out. And that's more than Lyndon Johnson could have done.

It was Jack Kennedy and Lyndon Johnson that got

us into it; it was Dick Nixon that got us out. He had opened China. Now, I've said some things about that, but what stands out is he did open China. It had to be done. Nixon did it. And Nixon had established a policy of détente with the Soviet Union, which was a big step forward in the Cold War, because it meant you could start to finally put some lid on the arms race. Before détente, it was just, "We build, you build; you build, we build." And it was just escalating up to these incredible figures—forty thousand nuclear warheads on each side, and what have you. It was Nixon who put a stop to that. He had the first arms control treaty in history that had some real effect. What followed, when Reagan made the deals with Gorbachev and with Communism finally falling down—we've got Dick Nixon to thank for that. Yeah, I think he deserved to be reelected.

Q: So, when you began the Nixon biography, you were a sort of a visceral detractor of Nixon?

A: Detractor? I was a Nixon-hater all my life. Oh, very, very much so. I thought that the man had no redeeming quality whatsoever.

Q: None?

A: None. The total lack of spontaneity in the man, everything was calculated. The only criteria for making a decision is "What's good for Dick Nixon?" and so on. And I believed all those things. And, to some extent, I still believe them. I mean, some of those things are true. But he rose above that.

Q: So you came out of the project as a begrudging admirer?

A: I wrote three volumes on this guy. Believe me, I didn't want to write about Dick Nixon. My editor said, "You've got to do it." And I said, "No, I don't even like the guy. I hate the guy." And my editor said, "Where else would you find a bigger challenge?" That caught me. So, it cost me ten years of my life. Three volumes on Nixon, about six hundred to seven hundred pages to each volume. The last line of the third volume is "When Nixon resigned, we lost more than we gained." And I never in this world could have dreamed that I could come to such a conclusion as that. But I did. It's the conclusion I came to.

He did a lot of good things. Did a lot of bad things. He deserved what he got. But he deserved reelection in 1972, also.

Q: What was the effect of that sweeping 1972 victory of his in the second term?

A: Well, typical of Nixon, the morning after the election he was angry. He called in Bob Haldeman and said, "Now, we're going to get rid of all of these people. We're going to get everybody's resignation right now." And Haldeman said, "Hey, boss, we just won an election. These people were out there campaigning for you. This is your team." No, Nixon said, "We're going to get rid of them. I want to have their written resignations on my desk."

Q: You mean his cabinet and his secretaries? Why did he want that?

A: He wanted the power over them. He wasn't going to accept all of those resignations, but he wanted them to know that he had the right to demand it. That's what it comes down to. And he came out of that tremendous victory so angry at the Democrats and at his favorites to hate—the *Washington Post,* the *New York Times,* and the liberal press, as he saw it—that he said, "We're going to get them now." It was a famous line, "We're going to get them down on the ground, Chuck"—this was to Chuck Colson—"we're going to get them down there, and then we're going to put our foot on their neck and then we're going to twist, and they're going to pay. Those bastards have been out there all those years after me, and now they're going to pay."

Q: So, here he comes now, he has carried everything but Massachusetts, and he's got all the power he wants, and he's going to crush his opponents.

A: Yes, that was the anger, that was the first thing. But he also had something else—and this is why I think he deserved reelection: He had a building policy in mind that was so big that he dared to call it "the New American Revolution." Everybody's forgotten that now, but, at the start of Nixon's second term, that's what he was pushing.

He was going to go for welfare reform. Think how long we've had to wait for that to happen. He was going to go after energy independence. He was going to go after black empowerment, putting money into the cities so that black entrepreneurs could start businesses. And it goes on. It's quite a long list. As a matter of fact, it's a list of what's been on the political agenda for the last twenty-five years.

Q: And all that was derailed?

A: He was going to put this through, and, of course, it was all derailed from the minute that the gavel went down at Senator Ervin's hearing.

Q: Do you think he had a premonition of what was going to happen to him during the second term? I mean, he never learned the great lesson in Washington, which is that the cover-up is, most times, worse than what you're covering up.

A: Eisenhower told him at a cabinet meeting in 1958—I've got the notes on this—Eisenhower turned to Nixon and said, "Listen, if you ever get caught in something, don't get cute and try to cover up, because if you do, you're going to get yourself so tangled you'll never get out of it." And that's a direct quote. Well, obviously, Nixon wasn't listening.

On the other hand, he didn't have a lot of choice.

People ask, once the existence of the tapes came to be known, why didn't he just take them out on the White House lawn, and call in all those reporters and say, "Watch, you sons of bitches," then pour some gasoline on those tapes, light a match, and he's home free, right? He didn't do that, because those tapes were his best defense. Now, Nixon knew what his administration had done. Nixon knew how vulnerable they were. Nixon knew what the results of deep, serious investigations were going to be. It was going to be a lot more than just breaking into Daniel Ellsberg's doctor's office, and it was going to be a lot more than the Watergate caper. There was a great deal out there that had to be hidden.

For Nixon, the defense was in the tapes, because he could see what the end of all this is going to be. He saw himself standing in the Senate dock, tried, being impeached. Then his lawyer would say to the Senate, "Gentlemen, you've heard what the prosecution has said. Now, I want you to hear what the president said to John Dean when John Dean said that it's going to take a million bucks to cover this thing up." And he hits the tape recorder, and the tape says, "But, John, that would be wrong." Boom, he hits the stop button. "Senators, I rest my case."

So long as Nixon controlled those tapes, they were his best defense, because he could use them selectively. Of course, it didn't work out that way.

Q: The fall of a great leader, eh?

A: That reminds me, because I write about these great men, I very often get asked, "What's the secret of leadership?" And my only answer to that is "I'm damned if I know, because they all have different ways." MacArthur's way was certainly different from Eisenhower's, which was certainly different from Nixon's, which was certainly different from Churchill's, and you can go on and on with that.

But there's one quality that all great men share, and that's luck. Napoleon spoke to it. He was asked what qualities he was looking for in his generals, and he said, "Just one—that they be lucky." Well, Jimmy Carter was unlucky. And, in a lot of ways, I think Bill Clinton is unlucky. Peace and prosperity can't compare to war and destruction and making decisions that affect the whole world.

Q: But that's crazy, isn't it? That's totally upside down.

A: Well, that's human. That's the way we are.

Index

Index

World War I, 61, 62, 76, 171, 191,
205
  Civil War comparison, 74
  as historical dividing line, 160,
163, 167, 206
World War II, 61, 62, 76, 177, 179,
180, 184–209, 218
  D-day as pivot point, 209
  issues at stake, 205–6
  specialness of U.S. troops,
199–208

  transformation of West by, 114,
123
writing skills, 155, 156, 169

yellow fever epidemics, 150
Yellow Hand, 100, 101, 182
Yellowstone National Park, 124
York, Sergeant, 171
Yorktown, Battle of, 47

Roger Mudd is a veteran television journalist whose long and distinguished career has taken him from national affairs correspondent on CBS to co-anchor of NBC's *Nightly News* and then to essayist and correspondent for *The MacNeil/Lehrer NewsHour*. His reporting has won him numerous awards, among them two Peabodies, five Emmies, and a special award for distinguished Washington coverage for *MacNeil/Lehrer*. Currently, he hosts the History Channel, which is the fastest-growing cable channel in the United States. Mudd's fascination with American history goes back to his boyhood: He holds undergraduate and graduate degrees in American history—he was even pursuing a doctorate until his career at a local newspaper drew him toward journalism—and he taught history in his first job out of college. In his free time, he enjoys reading books on a wide variety of historical subjects.